Overcome AD-versity

Overcome AD-versity

How to Put Persuasion Power in Advertising

Barry Milavsky

||BEP

BUSINESS EXPERT PRESS

Leader in applied, concise business books

Overcome AD-versity: How to Put Persuasion Power in Advertising

Copyright © Business Expert Press, LLC, 2024

Cover design by Andrea Katwaroo, designcovers.ca

Interior design by Exeter Premedia Services Private Ltd., Chennai, India

First published in 2024 by
Business Expert Press, LLC
222 East 46th Street, New York, NY 10017
www.businessexpertpress.com

ISBN-13: 978-1-63742-610-4 (paperback)
ISBN-13: 978-1-63742-611-1 (e-book)

Business Expert Press Marketing Collection

First edition: 2024

10 9 8 7 6 5 4 3 2 1

Description

Understanding the psychological bases for effective advertising is the key to creating advertising that has persuasive power. This book thoroughly explains ad development from inception through performance in the market. It offers useful ways to improve advertising, giving it more power through a deeper understanding and focus on the psychology of the target audience.

The book is instructional in its step-by-step approach, with practical insights to help demonstrate concepts and achieve better results. Insider lessons from a veteran of Madison Avenue, with psychology credentials, explain the whys and hows for practical advertising solutions. Learn the difference between product attributes and benefits; how to write a creative strategy; how to make advertising believable using psychological triggers; which advertising formats and styles work better and why; and how to evaluate ideas and see results from advertising.

The book concisely takes readers through the elements of persuasive advertising, demonstrated by the author's fascinating real-life examples with well-known brands, to understand practical applications of these ideas. The book has many first-hand cases from the advertising industry including a detailed study on how Bill Cosby became spokesman for Jell-O, plus helpful counsel for retail advertisers.

This book teaches how to reduce wasted efforts, giving ads more power. You'll learn how to create an advertising campaign, what to look for as leverage in the process, and how to evaluate the work. This book offers easy-reading, constructive counsel.

Keywords

psychology; brand; purchase behavior; strategy; believable; leverage; creative

Contents

Preface

This book is to help managers understand the process of putting advertising together; to learn to overcome the obstacles in developing advertising that works; to use proven techniques to add power to messages; and to reduce the risks that come with making a public statement meant to motivate audiences.

It should help those who manage the process of advertising more than for those who simply create the end messages, although it should be helpful for both. We will go through these challenges from understanding the product, to defining the need, to the advertising message, reviewing each element that is needed to make ads more persuasive resulting in advertising with more power to change minds.

While the focus here is on advertising, the process and frameworks that are outlined will function for any persuasive message in any medium. Understand the product, the target of the message, what you want to achieve, and what is needed to do so. Ads are not effective if they just show up, your message should have persuasive power; the more persuasion, the more power.

I have drawn on my own experiences and used examples I have been directly involved with because I know the process that went into creating those ads. I am reluctant to draw on someone else's work because I don't know the dynamics or conditions that went into the creation of those ads. Making assumptions is no way to gain clearer understanding.

My work experience and my background in psychology gave me the base to understand the advertising industry differently and to formulate these elements that should help everyone else understand how advertising is put together. It isn't magic. It is applying the power and knowledge of social science, and it is quite logical, even when it appeals to the emotions. The author would like to thank everyone who kicked, goaded, and encouraged me to write this, particularly John Rea, Brad McKay, Alan Cantor, John Luciani, Greg, and Alex. I couldn't have done it without the heckling and cheering! Thanks!

CHAPTER 1

Introduction

Understanding the Challenges to Overcome in Creating Advertising

They say that someone who acts as their own lawyer in court has a fool for a client. No one tries to do their own open-heart surgery.

My friend Duane is an engineer and he told me he could take out his own appendix if he had to; but Duane has a PhD in biomechanical engineering and went through the astronaut training program, so I do believe Duane could do just about anything he sets his mind to. Very few of us are like Duane with his focus and learning capacity, even if our self-confidence can be excessively high and we believe our inflated self-assessments.

Work done by lawyers, doctors, or professionals such as engineers, architects, accountants, and others requires a deep intellectual understanding of their field embedded in their brain, in addition to highly developed and quickly accessed technical skills. Is advertising different?

Advertising is *applied* social science. It applies science from psychology, sociology, even anthropology, to determine the most robust and effective ways to persuade. Understanding the psychology gives advertising power. Being in tune with the audience's brain helps you use the right words and pictures.

People may think because they have seen advertising in print or video that it can't be too hard to create it yourself. Isn't advertising just pulling a cool idea out of a black box? How hard can it be? Isn't it like watching an actor playing a lawyer in a movie or a TV show, it seems easy enough. The actors look like they are doing the job even if they don't write their own lines. But since we have to create the lines, we better know what goes into it.

To overcome the challenges of creating effective advertising, we need intellectual understanding and discipline. We need highly developed technical skills. To know if it is effective advertising, we need a clear goal or standard to evaluate against. We also need an objective ability to judge the work because everyone else will be judging it even if everyone else has no basis to do so. There are many hurdles to overcome; many ways to get sidetracked. We will unravel the steps you should take, to take on the adversity that will be encountered and achieve the ad's goal.

The steps to follow to develop and evaluate powerful persuasive messages are consistent, no matter the product or service. **Step One** starts with understanding the product to be advertised, not just its physical nature but the context in which it is used. Most advertising instruction jumps past the product; however, understanding the product's most important benefit the way buyers do is a critical first step.

Step Two From the understanding in step one, the promise of what the product can do best should emerge. It becomes the basis for a roadmap to follow for the advertising to be developed. We define the target for the message, the goal we are trying to achieve with the advertising, what the product promises that target and why it should be believed.

Step Three is a consideration for how believable that promise is and what ways the message can be made believable. **Step Four** is often where people start; how to fashion that promise into a message that is understandable, provocative, and compelling to the target audience. **Step Five** is where that message is translated into a format to deliver to the intended audience. **Step Six** is the evaluation of those options and how well they fit the product. **Step Seven** follows the advertising idea through the approval process and the challenges it must overcome to get to **Step Eight,** which is the production of the advertising. The final **Step Nine** is a look at the results from the advertising.

This book examines and explains each step in the order they occur as the advertising message is built and evaluated. We will be using our understanding of psychology to add power to each step.

The thinking part behind each of these steps cannot be ignored. It creates the operating framework that an advertiser must have to sell their product or idea.

Most advertisers can develop an ability to use that framework to operate as second nature once they understand the process. These technical skills can be acquired with about 10,000 hours of focused practice if you already have world-class talent. Or, more practically, unless you are Duane, you hire experienced professionals for Steps Four, Five, and Eight.

You should learn some ideas here that can help smooth your advertising development process and improve the persuasiveness of your ads. These skills will let you know if you are on the right path.

The Infinite Monkeys theory proposes that if you had an infinite number of monkeys on an infinite number of keyboards, they would eventually compose the entire works of Shakespeare. These days people are thinking that with artificial intelligence (AI) instead of monkeys, they might solve their advertising needs and do it faster with less of the monkey side effects such as constant chattering, throwing of feces, and climbing up on things.

Unfortunately, to understand whether the output from AI or the monkeys has any value or not, you need to be able to assess it against some standards for effectiveness. The goal is not just to make something, but to make something that delivers on its objectives, something that works. Otherwise, you produce: "To be or not to be, that is the gazortenflap!" Generating options is useless without being able to determine which of those options works. The goal of this book is to give you those standards.

We will review how to develop a skill set to allow you to be able to assess and evaluate what has been created. This can be especially difficult if you have made the advertising yourself. Self-criticism is hard. Most of us believe that we, ourselves, are wonderful. It is challenging to see something you created from the objective point of view of another person. Our goal here will be to help by creating some standards for evaluation.

You will need to supply some ***projected empathy*** to experience a message the way someone else does. That means learning to see things in the way someone else does, think the way someone else does, and even feel the way someone else does. This takes a lot of discipline and practice.

Advertising is a message developed to sell or convince someone of something: to establish an idea, to purchase a product, or to simply support an idea. To persuade. Advertising's job is not to entertain or even to win awards. These may be a pleasant side-effect of creating advertising, but they are definitely not a goal and can be a distraction that diverts attention from the actual goal.

It is a tricky balance: to attract attention, get people involved in the message, and still make your product or service and its selling idea the central core idea of the message.

Advertising is a lure and most often does not close the sale. Advertising promotes immediate sales; it also builds a longer term relationship with customers. That relationship builds equity for the brand in the form of loyalty, trust, and goodwill, like a savings account. This ongoing conversation with the consumer is a form of brand wealth that can be drawn on to sustain the brand when it needs it. There is an immediate reaction to an ad and a slower building long-term positive attitude that should grow if the advertising is successful in getting that immediate reaction.

While we are defining things, one term often used and misused is "brand"—it has been made into mysterious, complicated idea. It is not. It is a name. It is what you make cumulatively of it as represented through advertising, marketing activity, and its product-line extensions. Branding and advertising are not the same. Advertising is one way to express ideas about a brand.

We will use the word "product" to describe what is offered in the advertising, whether it is a physical thing or a service or an idea. When we use the term "advertiser" we mean the organization that is the beneficiary of the message, it can be a manufacturer, service provider, franchisor, franchisee, individual business or organization.

The goal of this book is to explain the elements needed to train your brain to help in the development and evaluation of persuasive messages. Our assumption is that you know something about advertising. Nevertheless, we will take what you might know apart and put it back together in a more robust framework. It will be worth it.

The power of communications has always fascinated me. By telling someone something in a particular way you can change their minds, change their lives. Persuasion has power. It can start wars. It can end wars. It can be a social herding mechanism. Despite what you may like to think, you are always being herded. Advertising is just the commercial sheepdog.

What makes some persuasive messages effective and others not? I studied this in school, then in grad school. What did I get out of it? In grad school, I gave some undergrads electrical shocks while doing physiological psychology tests in the grad school basement. I did some research papers for learned academic journals that very few read.

Then I got a job at Young & Rubicam (Y&R) on Madison Avenue in New York City. At that time, it was the largest advertising agency in the world and Madison Avenue was at its height of economic power. I went to work in the industry of changing people's minds, testing the old maxim "in theory, there is no difference between theory and practice; but in practice there is."

Since that time, Behavioral Economics has come into being and into vogue. Madison Avenue was already practicing Behavioral Economics, but without the academic recognition and terminology. We already knew heuristically what academics later discovered. I will use some of the more recent terms to describe how problems are addressed, even if they are anachronistic at times.

Academics know a lot about how persuasion works from the outside, under controlled conditions. Those in the industry had already learned about many of the techniques and structures of persuasion in the competitive world by putting in their focused practice with many failures and a few successes providing the feedback for learning. The industry learned on the job what academics were studying.

To say there is any formula for successful advertising is to understate the complexity of the advertising development process. From the outside, typically, you only see the peak of the iceberg, the last 30 seconds of months of development. That can be deceptive. The seven-eighths of the iceberg that lies below the surface, the structural mass needed to get the iceberg peak visible above sea level, is hidden. You need to know both parts, not just the superficial to be effective.

The human brain is like that. You can use logic and reason things out when you need to, but for everyday life you rely on the operating framework that the reasoning part of your brain has already created. To speak a language, you assimilate the rules, the words, the grammar, and the style; but you don't think about these rules in everyday life, you just intuitively use them.

For fluidity, the language has to be incorporated into the fast operational part of the brain. When you are learning another language, depending on your age, it is often not loaded into the fast operational part but stored in the slower less everyday portion of the brain. You see people translating from one language to the other by slowly translating one word at a time because the words are not in their operational memory. We have the same issue with obscure words; if I used the English word "eleemosynary" in everyday speech I would get unknowing stares. Those who did know it would have to search in their brain, connecting fragments, trying to figure it out.

Think about the correct adjective order in English: we all use it; it is in the framework provided to our operating brain, we know it, but only few can articulate what it is.[*]

"Your two precious tiny worn engraved ancient yellow Roman gold ceremonial belt buckles" might sound correct enough, but the quantity of adjectives makes the description hard to follow because of the rule about our ability to comprehend quantities, which we will see later.

Similarly, we want a clear operating framework for making advertising, so we see things quickly, in a blink, and know if they are right or

---

[*]Adjective order in English is as follows: Article/possessive, quantity, opinion, size, physical quality, shape, age, color, origin/religion, material, type, then purpose.

wrong. Building fluency in advertising means incorporating the rules we will outline here, into your operational thinking. It is learning to speak advertising.

We do this for sports. Our coach makes us practice and practice until we can perform the sport "without thinking about it"—letting our muscles operate and do what they have practiced without interference with any conscious thoughts that might disrupt the flow. Amateurs practice until they get it right, Professionals practice until they can't get it wrong.

This is training the fast operational brain where muscle memory, and many other operational skills, are stored. It allows your body to move without having to consciously think about giving body parts instructions. Your actions become second nature. That is how experienced advertising practitioners roll. That is why repeated experience is valuable; it integrates the learning into operational reaction.

We want your logical brain to understand the framework and the elements you need to create and evaluate effective ads. How you can use psychology to make advertising more persuasive. Then we want to load that framework into your operational brain.

Technology has given many people the ability to put together messages that look a lot like advertising. Not using AI to create ads, just the usual software that allows the user to put words and some graphics together into some format, or to edit video from their phones into a short film.

The software allows people to make ersatz ads: maybe a graphic with some copy or a video with a product in it. But it doesn't have the right elements to give it persuasive power so that advertising doesn't work. It's just another of a slew of mediocre messages, or maybe a slough of mediocracy.

Don't conclude that advertising doesn't work for your product. Conclude that bad advertising doesn't work for your product.

When you ask AI to write a joke, the elements may be there, but the jokes just aren't funny.

Software (programs such as Indesign, Photoshop, and video editors) provides a delusion of adequacy allowing the user to think they made a persuasive message, "Oh look, I made an ad!!" when they just made the tip without the foundation. They are just an actor without a script in a bad movie. Just because you can make it, doesn't make it any good. You made a "gazortenflap!"

Remember it was the mass below the iceberg tip that sank the Titanic. That mass holds the understanding of the elements needed to make the sale, to effectively convince the target of the message. You need it to give an ad power and persuasion and not just make an imitation of an ad.

Writing an actual ad to be published or broadcast can be the easiest part of the process. The harder part is the reasoning and thinking needed before the "creative" work begins. This structured thinking helps you develop and evaluate the creative work. Without it, you are playing darts in the dark. You might hit something. Or you might do some harm.

As a business, advertising is developed in environments usually more complicated than those assumed in commentaries on advertising, which aim to entertain readers; we aim to explain the elements of the process with all its adversity and not fall to superficiality. I hope we are entertaining too.

Pundits commonly select famous examples to support their theories without understanding what went into making those examples. Anyone can cite the Apple "1984" commercial as a landmark commercial, but only a few, like Fred Goldberg who was managing the Apple account, can tell the real story behind the thinking and development process involved in creating the commercial.[1] The critics usually overblow the final impact and fail to report the difficulty of the development issues. This is creating a false myth. It makes a good story, but doesn't help others. We won't be doing that. This is not a book about popular culture. It is a book about understanding the elements required in developing advertising that works. We will dig into what needs to be done to create persuasive messages that work, not just do some superficial commentary.

Advertising is not done in a vacuum and rarely by one person. Most times a team of experienced experts is needed. Most of us are not human Swiss Army knives like Duane. The social context and the disciplines to get an effective ad completed are part of the development process you should understand.

We will work through the paradigm your logical brain needs to incorporate before you let loose your intuitive brain or your hired team to create ad ideas that work. Here's our roadmap:

- Understand the product beyond the superficial to find its leverage point or address an unmet need.
- Develop a communications strategy and its elements: purpose, target, promise, and support for that promise.
- What kinds of strategies work best?
- What does advertising need to be believable?
- How to develop effective ad creative. The techniques we use and why they work.
- Evaluate and assess advertising ideas from the buyer's view.
- Manage the advertising approval process: organizational and legal.
- Producing the advertising—the skills, coordination, choices, and how to improvise when adversity strikes (hint: it often does).

We'll use my real-life examples (some are famous, most are not), because I understand the adversity the ideas went through in getting developed, approved, and produced. We will also address the social science that went into them with power tips on how to improve the persuasiveness of your ads.

Advertising is very ephemeral and is soon forgotten. Few commercials or ads are recalled a year after they are aired. They are designed to fulfill a particular timely function. Campaigns are meant to last longer; those that last for years are the gold standard. They are like hit songs. You might remember some individual ads; campaigns are more memorable because they cumulate. You would probably need a cue or prompt to bring songs out of your long-term memory; we could do the same for ads.

Like most people in advertising, I have worked on hundreds of commercials and dozens of campaigns. Writing this has given me some cues to recall some of them. I may cue your memory as well. Ads, like songs, are mostly not hits. Most are long forgotten, but by following a few rules that help the long-term memory they can endure to help build brands, and that builds wealth.

Even if you are not creating your own amazing ads, or taking out your own appendix like Duane says he can, after reading this book you will have a better understanding of how advertising is put together, scientifically and artistically. If you are creating your own ads, it will help to get more effectiveness and persuasive power from your own efforts, to resonate with your customers and to avoid the waste created by bad advertising.

We will do a checklist for each chapter.

Key Elements for Chapter 1: Introduction

- There is more to advertising that there appears to be.
- Having a clear framework for what ads require makes it easier to evaluate them.
- Project empathy with your prospective target; understand their needs and feelings.
- Understand where your product fits with your target.
- Developing a creative strategy is like having a blueprint before you build your message.
- Whatever you say must be believable.
- There are many techniques and elements to making advertising that works.
- All ads should be evaluated against the strategy.
- Ads are created within an organizational structure and face adversity.
- Producing creative ideas can have unexpected turns.
- Duane can take out his own appendix, but everyone needs help making great ads.

CHAPTER 2

Understand the Product

Find the Key Product Benefit for the User
From a Product's Many Attributes

Advertising books rarely start with an assessment of the product. To holistically understand the entire advertising development process, we should start with what the advertising is going to offer. Otherwise, we are jumping ahead of ourselves by assuming too many factors that could have major effects on the resulting advertising. It might not be the most exciting part of the process, but it is necessary as a foundation for everything that comes next.

Every branded product or service (we usually call all offerings products to keep it simple) is more than it appears to be at first glance. There is a depth to it. There is a physical description; it has a brand name; there is a production or operational process to make the product; it has a function, that is what it physically does; it has a place in the user's life; it fits into a social setting; it has a price; it has a history of what it has done and what has been said about it. These, and many more, are all *attributes* of the brand, product, or service.

Not all these attributes have interest to your buyer. Fact is *most do not*. Advertising should never be wasted on attributes that do not have a motivating benefit for the buyer. This sounds obvious but we see examples all the time.

Let's start with the product's name, its brand. If your product already has a brand name, then you need to build a value into it. By value, we do not mean price. It can be quality; it can be any benefit.

If it doesn't have a brand name, then give it one. You will read a lot here about the value of naming things and the benefits that attach to that name. There is a lot of communication power in a name. Don't give it a description, give it a name. People confuse generic descriptions with names. What a product does is one thing; what it is called is something else, something more than what it does. We worked with a dairy to sell its dry milk powder combinations: we gave the name Protelac to their big, brown, industrial bags of the milk protein powder. We gave it a logo. Manufacturers then asked for Protelac. The brand offered varying levels of protein within its brand line. It was not sexy. It was not even consumer directed, but there was a halo of added value in asking for the brand by name. Protelac was not alone in getting this treatment; we did a range of industrial products.

Often brand names have initial connotations of their performance, like Crest toothpaste suggested the comparison of the whiteness of your teeth with the whitecaps on the *crest* of a wave. But soon after launch, the brand name has little or nothing to do with its original genesis and takes on an identity of its own, an identity that the marketer creates. We give our kids names such as Victoria or Victor but don't ask ourselves, "victory over what?" we just accept it as a name without thinking too much of the secondary meaning, connotations, or origins.

I have worked on too many brand names to count, invented many, saw many retire to the Hall of Forgotten Products, and even a few brand names that have come back to life later in another product entirely. The list is long because many products fail. You may only hear about the ones that end up floating above sea level, but there are many more that are sunk in the deep. I have heard that the success rate for new products is about 1 in 10, but who knows because failures are rarely publicized. There is an old saying that success has many parents; failure is an orphan. Even those orphans had names.

The brand name should be simple without any possible multilingual confusion associated with it. Don't think small, check out possible translation issues—we have the Internet! If you can own the URL, you can probably own the name.

An original name can be owned, whereas a description cannot. No matter how original the name, you need to make it stand for something. If it is a new word, it will take an investment of time and money as you teach customers what your brand means. There is a learning curve for prospective customers that can be speeded up by supported exposure to the name through advertising or you can wait and let it build slowly. The faster people know the brand, the faster they can make a purchase. Time that passes without the prospects knowing of the brand means potential sales lost forever. The trade-off is the investment cost of getting the name exposed and known through advertising versus the opportunities/sales lost because the brand is still unknown.

Once you own a brand name, you can build an identity for it. If it is a memorable brand name and the product fails, you can reuse the name. The cumulated messages that you issue become part of the public's impression of the brand name. With an original name, the brand can have its own URL (or .com) for a website. The brand name gives the product imagery and expectations. Once you brand something, you must live with it. It becomes part of the product. Be very careful with the name. Consider protecting it with a trademark or copyright. You should protect the brand name by identifying a generic description of the product (like Crest "toothpaste") so that the brand is clearly understood as its name. With any name, a logo should be developed for it. The graphic presentation of the name, that is its logo, telegraphs the name more than any word can. Imagine the name Coca-Cola without seeing it in its logo script in your mind's eye.

Using alternative spellings of a word may allow you to own a word for your product's branding purposes. Clean is not klean, is not kleen, is not klene, is not cleen, is not Mr. Clean. Whatever the name, make it easy to read and say. You will be using it a lot.

A name that is unique helps your brand separate itself from its competitors and stand on its own. An old Bob Newhart sitcom had a running gag with a rural local who introduced himself as "Hi, I'm Larry, this is my brother Darryl, and this is my other brother Darryl!" The ridiculousness of having two brothers with the same name was funny. It is not funny if a prospective customer confuses your brand with a competitive brand because your names are too similar to each other, and that customer buys the competitor's product.

The brand name doesn't have to be just one word, but shouldn't be more than three words chunked together. Three is generally the limit of how many things the human brain can immediately and easily recognize at a glance. A glance can be handled by the fast operational brain and the customer doesn't have to engage their slow brain to understand. Seven is the upper limit of this, generally, according to psychologist George A. Miller; but few can comprehend seven things if they are not laid out in an easy geometric configuration. It is the customer's fast operational brain that must quickly identify your brand and make a decision. Is the light red or green? Decide, and stop or go. There isn't time for the fast brain to think about it. It has to be simple.

There are more limitations put on the communication process by the receiver of the message than there are by the sender. You might be able to go on and on; but I won't listen. You get no points for passes, just for completions. The communications must be clear and simple if it is to be received.

The pharmaceutical companies are fond of creating their own words for brand names, often because that name must work in many languages around the world. Unusual spellings are also popular. In their case, the generic name of a drug can be a complicated, difficult-to-pronounce description, so even a complicated shorter brand name with rarely used letters like y or x or q is easier. The name has to be easy, especially if the product's marketing strategy is based on patients asking their doctor about the drug. The patients must be able to easily repeat the name to their doctor.

While the **fast brain** sees your product, information about a product will filter through to the **logical** portion of the consumer's brain and into their memory. The brain is a leaky place. Ideas conflate and merge, often without the consumer realizing it; so what you said may not be what the logical brain recalled. Think of their brain as having a collection of index cards of things they know and can be readily available for reference. If you are lucky, your product may have a card of its own in the consumer's mind. On that small card would be the product name and a few words about it. If you are lucky. The operational fast portion of the customer's brain is busy handing everyday needs, not storing complicated memories. It can also store unarticulated sensory feelings, smells, tastes, visuals, and sounds that are associated with these quickly sourced ideas. When you are driving your car, you likely don't remember much of your journey, but your fast brain was operating in busy traffic just fine.

You might be able to talk about your product for an hour or more. The consumer will only have a few top-of-mind words about it. Then if they are required to, they will have to dig for something prompted by the brand name that is otherwise in their slow brain, something that would be totally off-line for them in the instant they are making their purchase decision.

In our physiological psychology research, people who were physically excited by exercise often had their brain mislabel that elevated excitement. When they witnessed an aggressive challenge later, the excitement was transferred, and they responded more aggressively.[1] Their brain had a two-step process for interpreting the stimuli: the physical excitation was transferred by their operational fast brain into anger causing them to be more aggressive. In the lab, they never got time to think through (consult the slow brain) how they should react; they had to respond immediately. The fast part of the brain doesn't moderate itself well. Freud might call it "the Id without time for the Superego."

Daniel Kahneman found the same leaky process in people when he considered how people think, as he outlined in his book *Thinking Fast and Slow*.[2] In many experiments, he and Amos Tversky concluded that one part of the brain, the fast part, is operational, pragmatic, and intuitive. The other part, the slow part, is logical and reasons things through.

The slow part provides frameworks for the fast part to operate but the fast part is what we use every day to get by. Our fast operational brains don't refer or defer to the logical part unless we are forced to, perhaps when someone says "pay attention" or we are challenged by a problem that is too complex. The context we find ourselves in can also stimulate use of the slower brain. For example, being in a classroom, or getting instruction on something, even if from YouTube, or attentively reading a book like this one (I hope). Mostly, the slower brain is in a passive mode. Not so the fast brain. It is active all the time running your life. Some people have called this fast brain the "lizard brain" because it cues on our basic needs. But it is more than that.

One could argue that the notorious Milgram experiments on obedience, where subjects were driven to act sadistically, were successful because the experimenters consistently cut off the subjects' desire to use their logical brain and forced them to live in the moment.

We use this fast part of our brains to operate daily. If I ask you "What is 2 × 2" you can immediately answer "4." But if I ask you "What is 17 × 23?" you probably have to stop what you are doing and use some energy to concentrate and source your slower thinking logical brain to figure it out, maybe visualizing the calculation. The fast and slow parts of the brain are interconnected and can work together, but it takes some effort and energy to engage the slow brain.

One human survival technique we have evolved is to avoid making calorie-costly efforts to source that slow logical thinking. We only do it if we must, either because the need is presented or the environment that we are in requires reference to that energy-expensive phase of our thinking. It is not that we are lazy; we just don't like to waste energy we might need later.

Like in the example about language, I don't have to think deeply about it to know that "I are" is wrong because my fast brain already has the language framework that has been learned and provided by the logical, slow part of my brain. There, I have learned the structure: "I am. You are. He is." and so on. Or that the "gray bad big wolf" just sounds like the wrong order and leaves one thinking "that person doesn't speak English" or they haven't got the full framework in their fast brain. The information is there, but it is not consistent with the framework.

When we use words or constructions, not on an everyday use, they are hiding in the slow brain. We only like useful operational information in the operational fast brain.

The habits, opinions, and attitudes we have learned get loaded into the fast intuitive brain for quick use when we need it. We need to know whether to fight or flee without thinking too long about it. Is some new stimulus an opportunity or a threat.

Most advertising only reaches the fast brains in our prospective customers, so we need to tune our advertising communication to how the fast part of the brain operates. No future perfect or pluperfect subjunctive in your advertising copy, please, or complex logic.

The right kind of stimulus and repetition can get through the fast brain to the slow brain, for the slow brain to process your product's benefits. Ideally, then, the slow brain can establish an operating framework that the fast brain can use that includes the product. But the fast brain is the gatekeeper. We have to talk to it first.

Now that we understand what part of your prospective customer is seeing your product. How do they describe, see, and use your product in their fast brain, if at all?

Not all the product attributes are useful to the buyers. Most are not. We define the useful ones as **product benefits**. Some of these benefits are motivating and unique to your product. Some benefits are generic; that is, these same benefits are provided by all products in your competitive category, to one degree or other.

All soaps clean; all restaurants serve food; and so on. These provide the source for the primary demand for the category. Advertisers need to focus on the product benefits that create the secondary demand for purchase of *their* product, which *differentiate* the product.

Marketing activity that focuses on the category benefits only helps your product proportionately to its share of the market. That is, if a brand has 50 percent of the sales in a market, stimulating category demand typically will benefit that brand with 50 percent of the sales created. If you are not the leader, spending time and effort on benefits that are generic to the category actually helps your competitors more than you. If you have a 20 percent market share, 80 percent of your advertising spending against a category benefit will be wasted. You will get only 20 percent of the impact you hope for. Blame that on the consumer's leaky fast brain for not being sure of the brand.

Sometimes the best benefit to focus on is not even your physical product itself, but your product is the mechanism to do or get something else. That something else may be the real motivator for purchase. This is not limited to just perfumes or cosmetics that are used to attract others. Think about the secondary impact of product use or purchase.

Years ago, I was giving a lecture at the Wharton School of Business at the University of Pennsylvania and asked the large undergraduate class in the lecture hall for a product they thought was dull and every day. The idea was for the class to understand how to develop a creative strategy that could lift a product out of its dullness. Anyone can tell you something exciting about a product that is already exciting; but it takes some thinking to make something dull as dishwater into something really interesting.

Among the branded products yelled from the crowded lecture theater was *Joy dishwashing liquid*. This struck everyone as a suitably unsexy product; functional, every day, boring, and associated with doing an unpleasant chore. I didn't know at the time, but 10 years later, I would be responsible for Joy's advertising. Things have a curious way of coming around in a circle. That day at Wharton, it was just a random selection in a group exercise.

The students' slow brains had been ignited by the context of sitting in a lecture theater listening, somewhat attentively, to some ad guy from New York. A lecture hall is supposed to be a place where you go to learn something new. The class discussed the product as best as they recalled, what it looked like (liquid, clear, golden, came in a yellow squeeze bottle) and what it did (cleaned dishes). Then they discussed how, as a *detergent*, it was not the same as the leading dishwashing liquid *soap*, Ivory, which evolved from the Ivory Soap franchise. Ivory branded bar soap was the starting point for Procter & Gamble's consumer-packaged goods empire.

The class discussed how detergents, like Joy, were chemicals (surfactants) that dissolved grease and therefore did a better job cleaning than soaps because soaps were derived from fats, so soaps could leave a film. There must have been some of the class that had taken courses in chemistry.

This was a good starting point. We went through a lot of the attributes of the product in addition to being a detergent: convenient squeeze bottle, clear golden liquid, lemony smell, price, even the bright yellow bottle. These attributes all provided differentiation from opaque, white ivory. Then we discussed which differences offered a benefit to the customer, not just a difference. There should be a benefit to the consumer in that difference that is enough to motivate a consumer to buy it.

The class felt that there would be a small noticeable difference in the cleaning, demonstratable to the touch and the eye, because there would be no film left behind like from a fat-based soap. This would leave dishes cleaner from a detergent, like Joy, than they would be from a soap. These kids were smart. They were Wharton students, after all. I reminded them that small differences can be magnified with advertising. (Remember this; it is important.)

They were completely unaware of Joy's advertising. I told them that Joy's advertising claim was that it cleaned right down to the surface of the plate, leaving no film. There was a collective patting of oneself on the back by the class.

Leaving no film was an excellent benefit and one that could be demonstrated visually. In fact, the Joy commercials at that time showed a woman looking at her reflection in a plate that had just been washed in Joy to show how clean the plate was—like a mirror. It demonstrated the end benefit as visual proof. By end benefit we mean the resulting benefit after product use.

This is what we call a strategic graphic, or a strategy visual. *A graphic proof is immensely more persuasive than a verbal claim.* The human brain processes visual information immediately in the fast part of the brain. Verbal information needs to be decoded to be understood, which might only take a moment, but it is not immediate, and it might take some effort. The fast brain is kind of a sieve that filters out information that is challenging or not necessary.

After demonstrating the end benefit of cleaner plates, the commercials go on to provide a social benefit, what the industry calls an **end-end benefit**, something over and above the physical benefit. The product creates an end benefit after it is used. But sometimes that product benefit can create and a secondary **end-end benefit**.

When we see the woman looking at her reflection, the voice-over announcer adds "isn't that a nice reflection on you?" to remind her that cleaning her dishes is not just a physical act but is also being personally and socially evaluated. That positive personal or social evaluation is over and above the job well done by cleaning a plate; it is an end-end benefit derived from the product's actual physical benefit, an extra bit of motivating persuasive power. The psychological satisfaction can be much more compelling than the physical delivery of the product performance. (Yes, commercials were also done with men cleaning dishes, but later.)

As detergents' share grew in the marketplace, gentleness to the hands became a counterattack benefit for the liquid dish soaps to make detergents seen as harsher. Those old enough might remember "dish pan hands" and "you're soaking in it" advertising campaigns for brands in the category. Even though the category has largely been supplanted by dishwashers, we can learn from the advertising claims dialogue that took place between products in this category. Products addressed unmet consumer needs to create competitive differences.

The process we went through with these students is the same process that everyone developing advertising should follow: looking at the product, then sifting through the many attributes to get to the key end benefits, then determining which of those benefits are more motivating for your potential purchasers. To do that you need to ask a lot of questions to purchasers of the product or service, and you need to listen closely to what the product users say.

For Jell-O pudding (JOP), we learned that parents made pudding for their kids so that the kids would consume more milk. Our commercials always showed a pitcher of milk next to the product. The product was a catalyst for something else the purchaser was trying to do: build strong bones for growing kids by getting calcium into them. That's four steps to get to the real benefit, pudding-to-milk-to-calcium-to-bones; the connection of milk to bones had been well established in the parents' minds. It was an accepted belief for almost everyone. Many products are catalysts like that, particularly those for health and appearance.

For every product or service, there is a wide range of utilities, ways that the product creates impact for customers. Sometimes it is not the most obvious physical one that drives sales.

Manufacturers, retailers, and distributors usually focus almost all their attention and their efforts on getting their product to the market.

I have attended many product development meetings where endless conversations reviewed ingredients, packaging, sizing, price implications, product processes, and even commodity availabilities. Even minor ingredients such as Gum Arabic and carrageenan have volatile markets and must be imported from somewhere, and that takes planning. Big commodities like coffee also need commitments for multiyear buys, future price hedges, and so forth. It is not a simple thing to bring any product to the market. We visually see the tip of the iceberg but there is a lot more to it.

As a result, when manufacturers think about the product, their focus can be to look backward at where the product came from, because that's where all their efforts have gone. I have visited factories, warehouses, and worked in client restaurants. Owners and managers extol the efforts, operations, and processes that they have had to go through to achieve their products; how their technology works; how long they have been in business; and so on. They are proud of their achievements.

Most of the time, their customers don't really care about any of the advertisers' efforts. The consumers only want their end-benefit. Don't confuse your process with sales results.

After years of working on quick service restaurant (QSR) advertising, I can usually enter a QSR and tell you whether the manager is doing a good job. I base it on how the customers are being served. The manager's job and responsibilities might focus on the back of the restaurant: making sure supplies are ordered, staff is scheduled, quality of food and processes are maintained. There is a lot to manage.

As an advertising person, I only care about these things because they all affect the product that is delivered. I am downstream from the product creation and upstream from the customers. The customers don't see breakdowns in operations, staffing shortages, any of that. They just see slow service or badly prepared food.

The customer is only interested in the result, what we call the WIIFM (What's In It For Me). Why should they care about the operational challenges? They don't want to look at that other part of the iceberg below the surface. That is the manager's business not theirs.

The lesson: Don't have your advertising focus on everything *you do* unless you can pay it off with what's in it for the customer. Emphasize the customer part. *Your advertising is not about you, it is about your customers* and their satisfaction, their WIIFM.

I often use the line "Your job is easy; my job is hard" to remind people that others have no sympathy for issues you have with your processes. There is just the WIIFM!

It is hard to look at your product and see the multitude of ways it can be helpful to your customers unless you can put yourself in the product user's position. It's even harder sorting through those ways and choosing which one or ones to focus on. Make a list and cross off those that are not highly motivating. Keep crossing off the ones that are not compelling. The more you can get your choice down to one benefit, the easier it will be to communicate that benefit. Remember, the fast brain is twitchy and the index cards are small.

Few consumers are motivated by a catalog of product benefits; one strong end benefit works best. (See the Nobel story in the Appendix)

A good way to start is by creating an inventory of all the possibilities and then do a "so what" test to try to sift out the less powerful ones. If you challenge something about the product with "so what" and you don't get a compelling "really important" response, be like Marie Kondo and throw it out.

At this point, don't worry about the specific words you would use to describe the benefit to your potential buyers. Those will come later. Look at all the possibilities. Don't stop when you think you have the best. Keep going. Sort through them only after you are done and have completed the list.

As in the Joy example, understand how your product or service is used, its social setting, the psychological and physical needs it addresses. Your end users or purchasers are the experts in this, not the manufacturers. Talk to some customers. Ask why they buy it, listen to them, and how they talk about your product. You need to know how your product measures up against competitors in order to see if you have an advantage in some area.

Sometimes it is tough to speak with users. When I handled the national account for a major dog food brand, we obviously couldn't speak to the end consumers. We spoke instead to the purchasers, the dog owners, and categorized them based on their relationships with their pets. We grouped their attitudes toward their pets on a range from "surrogate child" to "livestock." The types of food that owners chose correlated nicely with this. The closer to surrogate child they considered their pet, the more the food had to resemble human food, and so on.

Surprisingly, many assessed their dog food choices based not just on whether the dog ate the food or not, but on the firmness of their dog's poop.

Most hungry dogs are not that choosy and will enjoy any food. They have to be trained to be fussy. The end benefit of "firm feces" was clearly not an advertisable benefit at that time with the social standards of the day and the conservative restrictions on what could be said on television; but it was great feedback and a goal for research in product development. It was not what product management had been aware of when we started speaking with customers.

When you are understanding the place your product has in consumers' lives, don't just look at the obvious attributes of the product. Widen your scope. More often, the psychological or social benefits can be more powerful than the physical ones. Most of us don't lead our lives looking for success and happiness at cleaning dishes, but we do constantly look for personal and social satisfaction and approval that can be derived from doing our tasks well, no matter how mundane.

Force yourself to make that inventory of your product attributes. Be as thorough as possible. Make a list so that you don't just jump to a conclusion and miss something.

Then eliminate anything that is at parity to your competitors.

Taking your product buyer's point of view (an exercise in projective empathy), prioritize the relative appeals of the benefits that you haven't eliminated. Look for unique features. Think about why people come to the category and your product. It is very hard to stay objective but try to be.

Don't get stuck on semantics—for example, whether the taste of a product is great, excellent, or spectacular is not that important at this phase. Taste would be the differentiable benefit. You are preparing to write the blueprints for the tip of the iceberg. Worry about the specific advertising wording later when you are preparing the execution of the creative strategy, besides, those ad folks are good with catchy phrases and descriptions. Don't buy a dog and bark yourself.

You should end your exploration with a clear idea of why people come or will come to your product and what they currently think about it. Be objective. You should understand their attitudes and their beliefs about the product.

All this should result in a simple sentence such as "Our product XXX is better at XXX." It should not be a compound sentence with caveats or conditions. Sounds simple, but simple is hard.

Hopefully, this should be a voyage to rediscover your product from the perspective of the buyer.

Keep it simple and you will be able to effectively communicate your product's strength. The more complicated the benefit, the less likely your customers will understand what you are offering. Their fast brain isn't too smart or too interested in your product.

Don't try to nuance this; leave that until you are crafting the message to go to prospective buyers.

Key Elements of Chapter 2: Understand the Product

- Look at your product from the point of view of your users.
- Humans have two types of brains: fast operational ones and slow logical ones.
- All advertising is directed at the fast operational portion.
- The challenges you have had in producing the product probably don't matter to buyers.
- The only attributes that matter are the ones that benefit your customer.
- Sort through product benefits for the ones that matter most. Ask as many questions as you can.
- Ignore benefits that are common in the category where you complete.

- Find benefits unique to your product, not shared in the category.
- Look for possible end-end benefits that provide social or psychological benefit.
- Find one benefit that has the most appeal to customers.
- Keep your benefit statement simple and direct.

CHAPTER 3

The Elements of a Communication Strategy

The Strategy Is the Blueprint to Building a Persuasive Message

To make persuasive advertising that works, we don't try to wing it on the fly. It is not a flash from the fast brain. We engage our logical brains and put them in control of the direction for the process. We will be designing the treasure map to what we want to achieve to focus our efforts.

To guide us, we construct a template based on an argument flow that should lead to the end benefit. It will be the framework, the paradigm, the blueprint for all communications to persuade people with our selling idea and convince them to buy into it.

We call this the **communication** or **creative strategy**. It is constructed by the slower logical brain to fit nicely into the fast, intuitive brain's way of thinking. The same way grammar and style from the logical brain is the framework for our everyday language. The creative strategy will provide the direction to create the persuasive expression that is to be shared with potential customers.

Just because we are using our logical brain to develop the strategy doesn't mean that all selling ideas must be logical or that emotion has been eliminated to the selling process. Emotion can logically be employed to improve selling effectiveness. We know that when people are emotionally charged, they are more open to receiving and considering ideas.

Why do we want to address the customer's fast brain? It is always on. It is the immediate interface people have with the world, and it is the gatekeeper that allows information to be perceived and assimilated.

The slow brain requires effort and self-control to turn on. Laziness in thinking is one of humanity's operating constants. The slow brain uses energy that we would rather conserve. Advertising is a lure to gain interest from the fast brain. If advertising can effectively engage the fast brain, there will be opportunities to engage the slow, logical brain after the message has passed through the filters and resistance that have been set up in the fast brain.

Virtually every professional advertising person uses a paradigm such as the creative strategy that we will explain here. The creative strategy tells you what you want to achieve and how. Until you know where you want to go, you are wandering in the wilderness. The strategy forces you to use your logical brain to create the framework focus for the intuitive fast brain to initiate creative message development that can resonate with buyers. So, how to begin?

The best way to change someone's mind is to start with what they currently believe and use it as a leverage point.

By starting with what people already believe, an argument is less threatening and won't immediately activate their defense mechanisms, rejection, and counter arguments that will shut out the proposition altogether. Confrontation simply creates confusion and resistance. We need to create negotiation when we want to advance our propositions.

People's first reaction to new information is to defend their current beliefs.[1] It is better to be in a discussion than to be in a battle. People also change the topic, sometimes without realizing it.

Kahneman confirmed that and noted that when you ask people difficult questions, they will often answer another question and not the question asked, even if it is only remotely related, to satisfy the questioner. Usually, this is a question that is much easier to address and doesn't require evaluation by the logical brain. The response is made without the responder noticing the substitution of another question. This is normal politician behavior, sometimes consciously to avoid a difficult issue, but it is also done by everyday people when confronted with a difficult question that requires analysis and thought. Better to respond from something handy. I don't know how many times in a staff meeting, when I asked if a task got completed, in response, I received a litany of steps in the process someone had taken to try to get the task done. That was not the question and was often a clear cue to tell me that the task did not get done. Nevertheless, the responder thought they were answering the question.

That leaves direct or difficult challenges leading to obfuscation and no positive result.

Most of what we believe, we hold in our intuitive fast brain ready for immediate use. We rarely defer to our logical slower brain unless it has been cued. We use the fast brain because we need to access our opinions quickly to express them. Anyone or anything that challenges those held opinions gets a reaction, usually defensive, not a reasoned response. We might dismiss this as emotional, but it is pragmatic. Our immediate opinions can be inconsistent with each other. That doesn't seem to bother us or create dissonance requiring resolution because the opinions or beliefs are not all processed through the logical slow brain.

To convince a prospective buyer of your persuasive message, you need to work with their current intuitive beliefs and find ways to evolve those beliefs. People tend to refute or avoid information that is dissonant to their held beliefs. Avoidance is something social media and cable news channels have exploited well. We redirect our media exposure habits to information that only reinforces current beliefs. This behavior uses less energy. We imitate the fast brain's gate-keeping preferences that can filter information and do not require us to access the slow logical brain.

Advertisers can open a door to the slow brain through the fast intuitive one. To get to that door, recognize what the current beliefs are about your category, brand, and product.

To fully participate in our strategy building exercise, take a piece of paper and use the headings for each section to create a form to fill in with your answers or best guesses for your own advertising strategy.

There is a logic to this process you will see even more clearly as we go through.

What Do People Currently Believe About the Product (or Category)?

This is the first task in creating a communication or creative strategy for your advertising: understanding what the consumer's currently held belief is. It might be about your brand, your product, your competitor's product, about the category, about a problem the product can solve, or even about what benefit you are thinking about offering as the focus of your sale. It might be positive or it might be negative. It should have come up as part of your examination of your product from the buyer's point of view that we went through in the previous chapter.

This belief is the foundation where you will build your creative strategy. It is the pivot point that leads to the rest of your strategy. Your strategic goal will be to evolve that belief by promising something that responds to needs within that belief. This allows the consumer to *adjust* or evolve their belief while not feeling that the belief is being directly challenged. If prospects feel attacked, they will "fight or flee" by arguing against you or ignoring your message. They need a WIIFM acceptable to their current belief set as an incentive to open the door to an attitude change that can evolve though reaching back and getting revised input from the slow brain.

Understanding what people readily accept as a truth is not easy, yet it is the linchpin for your entire creative appeal. When we were introducing Ortega Taco kits and sauces for Heublein back in the 1970s, we judged that the accepted consumer belief was that Mexican foods were weird, not understood, had unknown ingredients, lots of peppers, were foreign, and were very, very spicy. Mexican food was classified as very different from more familiar foods, like hamburgers, that might be substitutes.

If we wanted Ortega tacos to be anything but a niche, ethnic product, we had to overcome that accepted belief to gain significant sales.

This led us doing a advertising, showing blondes, middle-aged Midwestern families, and nerdy little kids enjoying the product. We showed common ingredients such as hamburger meat, lettuce, tomatoes, and cheese going into a taco shell. The only thing uncommon and new at the time was the taco shell. The advertising was essentially positioning a taco as a crunchy hamburger. When you see people who may look like you, doing something a little different, it doesn't seem strange.

With today's ubiquitous success of Mexican foods, the old, accepted belief from the 1970s is almost hard to believe. It is a good example of how social and dietary change can happen. Little by little, not by confrontation.

If the accepted belief we had chosen for our strategy had been "tacos are for people of Mexican descent," or "use Ortega Tacos to feel more Mexican," our volume expectations would have been more regional, occasional, and much lower—limited to celebrations of Cinco de Mayo once a year. The commercials would have looked considerably different, probably with some mariachi music. So you can see how the accepted belief is the leverage point from which the advertising emerges.

When you start your strategy development, you need some honesty and perspective. The fast brain will be entrenched with opinions and want to fight or flee. You have to carefully guide around entrenched ideas to find some commonality to negotiate—making a taco look like a crunchy hamburger.

The accepted belief may lead your product to a strategy of differentiation if consumers feel all products deliver at parity.

It may be that a particular benefit is something that can differentiate you, but your product is seen as weak. That leads to a strategy to strengthen the perception of the product quality or create more importance to some feature of the product.

Whatever the accepted belief you choose to initiate your strategy, it should be one that the majority of your prospective buyers would quickly agree to and endorse. This belief doesn't have to be universally held by everyone (what belief is universal?), but the more people who believe, the more buy-in you will get for your strategy.

Who Is the Target for Your Advertising?

Many retailers I have spoken with will say "Everyone is a potential customer," which might be a nice sentiment when serving people, but when aiming your message "everyone" is far too wide and imprecise. There is an old saying in advertising: "Half the money I spend on advertising is wasted; the trouble is I don't know which half." It is often attributed to John Wanamaker of Philadelphia, owner of the first department store in the United States.

The entire objective of defining a target is to increase the possibility of getting your message to prospects with a propensity to buy the product, not all people. It is like using a magnifying glass and sunshine to focus the rays to create heat and power. The better you can aim, fewer of your advertising dollars will be wasted. You want to fish where the fish are; this bears repeating (bears like fish).

No matter how tightly you focus your aim, you will invariably speak to many more people. The target to aim for are the core *customers who will build your business*. So, who are they?

Define your target in every way you can think. Use demographics such as age, education, income, and other variables, but not these alone. Don't use the media definitions alone. Try to imagine a customer to get a three-dimensional feel for them, what they are like, preferences in other areas, attitudes, and long-term desires. These people do not have to be current customers, but they should be potential customers who would be happy using your product. Again, there should be some aspect of your product that is highly relevant to this target. It is not "everyone." Even if everyone uses the product, the brand purchase decision may be made by only a subset of them. We want to reach that key purchase decision maker.

I mentioned that we used research to categorize dog owners based on their attitude toward their dog. We have done similar correlation analyses with car owners to sell a gasoline company's higher-octane gas. People's relationships with their cars varies a lot: from an old used car, a beater that just gets the driver from point A to point B, to drivers with muscle cars that are an expression of their personality and levels of testosterone, and groups in between whose car is for status, practicality, personal affection, and luxury. If they have given their car its own name, they have a different relationship as well.

We called this analysis, "autographics" (we in the industry like cute names, and it makes the concepts more real and more memorable). Think about the users of your product and how they can be grouped.

Most categories can be sliced into segments like this. These kinds of analyses can be done if you have the data. If you do, regression analyses and all kinds of data-based analytic techniques can be used to better define and group your optimal target. You might find, like we did with dogs and cars, that behavior changes with the segments. You might notice that neither dogs nor cars actually purchase anything. They have purchasers who do it for them while the pets provide influence.

We can also use programmatic online ads delivered by algorithm that seek out potential buyers based on personal profiles, web behavior, preferences, browser history, demographics, and so on. However, this book is about getting the message right, not about media buying; we will leave programmatic and predictive algorithms aside. If your message is right, informed delivery can only make it more effective by having the right message appear in the right place at the right time.

As a mental exercise, picture your target. What are they like? You might even have an imaginary conversation with them. If you can, find a real one for real conversation.

It will help you make assumptions about what they might believe about the product or the category it competes in. Empathize with their point of view as best you can to understand their motivations. Even think about some of their other life decisions: what kind of car do they have, what kind of job do they have, what kind of music do they like, are they savers or spenders, are they conservative or liberal, and so forth. You might even give them a name that makes them seem even more real.

With a large advertising budget, we would often convene focus groups to listen to how our target spoke about the brand or product and the language they used to talk about products and how they fit into their lives. Their language can be helpful in tailoring your message to them in the right way. We always want to talk to them in the same way they talk about the product and its uses. Speaking to them like they speak adds credibility and clarity to the message.

When you create a typical imaginary target, you start to see your customer as more of a real person than if you just look at demographics. It helps your fast brain understand the customer; it helps you create your heuristic model of your target.

The target doesn't necessarily need to be an end buyer of the product. Advertising has many other uses.

Sometimes the target for advertising can be stakeholders of the business. We changed one regional QSR client's advertising by changing their media buy from radio and outdoor to include television as a way of reaching more eaters, but there was a collateral benefit to the client. They sold more franchises. Potential franchisee investors saw the QSR chain as being bigger with more growth opportunities because they saw advertising on TV. These new franchisees were a different kind of buyer.

One large public organization client was facing a major labor disruption and chose to eliminate a talking point in the negotiation by using advertising to take the high ground with the public. They felt that with public support for the work the organization was doing, it would reduce the leverage their workers might have in bargaining.

You might have a message for shareholders or a message about corporate responsibility that has little to do with selling product but a lot to do with creating positive imagery for the corporate brand. You might want to increase share prices. Advertising can build equity as well as building sales.

Whatever the target you choose, your advertising will also open the door to public scrutiny from many sides. Be prepared for this.

The indirect receivers of your media are called "spill." You may get a lot of spill. To minimize it, define your target thoroughly because you will be addressing your advertising to them.

What Is the Goal for Your Advertising?

If you have no clear goal, you cannot evaluate results. Advertising effectiveness can be difficult to assess at the best of times; without a clear goal, it is virtually impossible. Even without an evaluation mechanism in place, beyond watching for sales, a clear goal should be established.

In general, advertising's goal is to persuasively convince someone of something. It is not always direct to make a sale. There are many goals you can establish for your advertising before you start creating any ads. Here are a few examples to stimulate thinking:

- Generate trial of your product or retrial (reactivate lapsed users). Retrial is often associated with a new improved version of the product as the product change can give permission for a lapsed user to return.
- Motivate customers to use up their household inventory (recipes and alternate uses).
- Create pantry loading (stock up today!) for potential future use.
- Shorten the existing purchase cycle to increase frequency of use or visits.
- Increase top-of-mind awareness (saliency).
- Increase the average check, the amount spent (trade up).
- Create a preference for a product with a long-term purchase cycle.
- Reassure users who have already purchased that they made the right choice.
- Create a more positive work environment by motivating employees and improving recruiting.
- Improve branding credibility by building a positive relationship with customers.
- Endorse a social responsibility.

There are many other such goals you can aim at. To prepare an effective message, you just have to pick *one*! You can't jump on your horse and ride off in all directions. Just one.

Make the goal a simple sentence, not a compound one with multiple goals. Trying to do more means failure. In a message of 30, 15, or 5 seconds, you must be succinct and clear. **Pick one or achieve none** (Now would be a good time to read the Nobel story in the Appendix).

Depending on what goal you have chosen, what you will promise your target can be very different. All communication should be focused on achieving that goal. For example, if you want to generate trial or retrial of your product, you might want to highlight a new product improvement, something that makes the product more appealing than it was or fixes something consumers felt was a weakness.

If you want to shorten your product's purchase cycle, you may want to feature usage ideas such as recipes or new alternative uses that create use up or talk about a high-value trade-in so that the prospect starts thinking about a shorter purchase cycle.

If you want to increase frequency of use or visits, you may use inducements such as bounce-back coupons, contests, or other techniques. With QSRs, we featured new menu items as limited time offers to improve the frequency of visits by creating some urgency to visit while the product was offered.

Keep in mind the purchase cycle for your product, that is, how long people take to be in the market to buy it again. Some purchases have long purchase cycles with a long consideration time in advance of the actual purchases. Some are lower price frequent purchases. Large purchases, such as cars, homes, or trips, can take a year or more for consumers to gather information and consider before taking any action. You might wish to add some incentives to fuel that consideration period and even shorten it.

Adding the word "repeat" to instructions on a shampoo bottle helped increase use-up and shortened the purchase cycle.

Making a sale is a transaction, a single event. Advertising is a continuing conversation with your customers. Keep the conversation going. Building a brand has a cumulative effect that pays off more and more over time.

What Do You Want Your Advertising to Promise?

This is the most important element in creating advertising. It is the pivotal idea that separates your product from others. Your lure. What are you promising to do for your target?

Advertising is an offer to interest the consumer into entering into a transaction. Most times the actual transaction occurs later. Transactions are an exchange, a bargaining. I offer you this and you give me that.

When the advertising tells you how wonderful a product is, it is enticing you by offering you something of benefit if you purchase or use the product.

The advertising message is brief: 30 seconds, a digital ad that comes and goes in a blink, a print ad that the reader scans, notes, and maybe reads, a billboard the driver goes by at 60 mph. The advertiser's selection of what to promise you to gain your interest is critical to the effectiveness of the advertising. What promise can motivate the target to start the transaction process? What's the WIIFM?

The offer may feature the product that you want to sell or it may be a top-of-the-line product that has "all the bells and whistles," even if you know the buyer will trade down from it to something more affordable.

The promise should be a simple declarative sentence: not complicated and not compound.

Generally, for a brand, this promise will not change, sometimes for years. Although some of the support reasons for the promise may change over time.

The promise should answer or address a consumer need by providing a solution.

For consumer food products, as an example, there are only four types of promises that products can deliver on. We group them as sensory delivery, body effect, convenience, and price.

Their effectiveness as benefits is in that order from strongest (sensory) to weakest (price).

Addressing them from the bottom up, *price* is the weakest because it can almost always be matched quickly by the competition, so it is a weak pillar to build on. Using a pegged or fixed price cannot be a long-term solution in the face of inflation.

Lowering the price can be a short-term enticement for trial, quick sales gains, or to react to competition. Beware of the fact that price reductions only work if there is a plan to return to the regular price.

Convenience relates to product form or delivery mechanism; it is harder for competitors to match this quality than it is to match price, but not impossible. Convenience gives a product a temporary time window of opportunity, but it can be difficult to defend.

All QSRs deliver convenience. McDonalds created immediate service; Wendy's invented the drive-through window for even greater convenience. Neither brand rested on this convenience benefit because both forms of convenient delivery soon became parity promises for everyone in the category. It took competitors some time to gain that parity; the time to catch up is a level of technological insulation for the claim, but it can be matched if a competitor believes that convenience is a valued benefit to offer customers.

By *body effect*, we mean that the product has an ingredient or ingredients that change how your body operates. The ingredient might be alcohol, caffeine, no caffeine, vitamins or minerals, low calories, no sugar, no high-fructose corn syrup, added omega 3, a keto formula, high fiber, Atkins formula, and so on. These formulations can be the key motivators for purchase of the product.

While these are benefits, they can also be equaled quite easily by competitors. Can you find salt without iodine in it? There might have been once when iodizing was an advantage, but it was quickly negated by almost all table salt becoming iodized. The same is true for many body effect claims. Adding or removing ingredients in a food product is not exactly rocket surgery. It just takes planning and reformulating.

For food products, taste, odor, look, or any benefit that *appeals to the senses* is the best area to create your product's promise. No other brand can taste, smell, or look exactly like yours. Even if customers can't tell your product from a competitor, you can claim uniqueness in its sensory delivery. Nothing tastes like a Coke, except in a blindfolded test. That doesn't stop claims for the uniqueness of the taste.

Many studies have shown that creating an expectation context for the product's sensory delivery can help immensely. Creating the right context can improve the product's sensory delivery. Many tests have shown that consumer preferences filter through their biases. For example, we rate the sensory delivery of the same wine better if it is in a bottle with a label that looks or sounds expensive, with a high independent rating, or a well-known designation. The same is true in the Coke/Pepsi challenges or beer taste tests. It is hard to tell one from the other without a label and the label can make all the difference.

This is the same process that we discussed in Chapter 2 about incoming physical data requiring interpretation before evaluation. The fast brain can provide context through its current beliefs.

Because the context for product consumption can be created through persuasion and relies on communication, it is where advertising can have the most impact.

While it might be easier to separate foods into four categories (sensory, body effect, convenience, and price), most nonfood products can also see a similar hierarchy in benefits.

Automobile benefits that deliver sensation appeal—the thrill of the ride, the great look, and the status—can rank higher than those that deliver body effects such as safety, extended warranties, and fewer emissions. The convenience of fewer repairs, easier to operate, local services, and so forth still rank higher than price. Notice that the more immediately the benefit is evident to the consumer the more persuasive that benefit can be. The here and now is fast brain territory.

A senior Toyota executive, a former client of mine, told me that he felt price should be sold by auto manufacturers based on the three Rs: Retail price, Repair cost (reliability and cost of maintenance), and Resell value. That's very logical but a difficult concept for most fast brains to understand when seeing advertising. The benefit is delayed over time, maybe years. The argument is, however, a strong one for a salesperson to make at the point of purchase to close the deal and reduce pricing discussions.

In developing your product strategy, look for the kind of promise that has the most enduring leverage and can be identified with the product. Try to avoid convenience and price. They do not sustain and can be matched.

Sometimes advertising doesn't talk about the key benefit. When we introduced Pampers disposable diapers in a foreign market, we avoided talking about Pampers' convenience, which was its primary benefit. With Pampers, there were no dirty, smelly cloth diapers to store and clean each day, no pins to wrestle to fasten them, and no need to check babies to see if they were dry. Pampers was so easy to use; it made mothers feel like they might be taking a short cut and cheating on their babies. That sense of emotional responsibility was a strong deterrent to gaining category trial.

We showed the convenience of disposable diapers without ever mentioning it. Advertising only talked about how Pampers kept baby's bottoms drier by wicking the liquid away. Leaving the baby's bottom drier was a demonstrable "end" benefit for baby (excuse the pun), reduced rashes, and an end-to-end benefit for mother of a happier, drier baby. Mothers were interested and committed to anything that improved their babies' lives. Convenience might have been the real purchase motivator, but it was not the best thing to promise. The emotional, sensory benefit trumped the convenience in our advertising.

Betty Crocker cake mix had a similar issue. When cake bakers only had to add water to the mix, they felt it was not really baking, so the recipe changed to have the baker add an egg. We sold the water-only version, sized down, as a quick snack called Snackin' Cake. It had less requirement for commitment because it was just a snack. Convenience was seen to reduce sensory benefit.

When there is a contest between technology and psychology, in marketing it is psychology that wins. That's where the purchase decision is coming from.

The point here is that the obvious is not always the best promise to lead with. The promise must be motivating and meaningful and give the advertiser more insulation from competition. There is a hierarchy to the power in promises. What the advertiser promises may not be the only thing the prospective customer takes away from the advertising.

Make the promise strong. Make it one simple sentence. No "ands" or "buts" in the sentence. Do not use "adsy copy" or evocative words in your strategy, leave those for the copywriter. Just focus on what the product does that makes customers want to buy. The important thing is to omit the unnecessary benefits. They cloud your communication by making it more difficult for the target to understand what the product promises to provide.

The more you can identify a unique promise, the more protection you have from competitors. The first product to promise something usually has more ownership of that claim than a competitor coming later. Of course, how widely that claim is disseminated plays a big part as well.

How Do You Support Your Promise?

What are the reasons why the product's promise should be believed? We have an entire chapter on being believed, but that comes later and evaluates the advertising message, not the strategy.

Here, we will address what attributes of the product support what the product promises to do. While advertisers may be tempted to create a long list of why the product performs its tasks, they should limit the support points to a maximum of three. People can't really comprehend more than three things in their fast brain, remember Miller's research. Once you get to three support points, additional points start to become weaker and weaker. A weak support point can undermine your overall promise by allowing prospects to argue with the weakest support point instead of the overall promise. If the promise conflicts with their belief, they will argue with a support point, not the promise.

All support points should link clearly to the promise, and you should expect them *all* to be mentioned or shown in the final advertising created.

Let's say you claim that your product tastes great. The reasons why it tastes great could be particular ingredients, a special manufacturing process, customer satisfaction, taste preference by experts, and quick delivery to the customer. The more specific you can make these points and the more they are exclusive to your product, the better. Specifics are more believable than generalizations.

Support points give the target reasons why they should believe the promise is true and purchase the product. Here are some examples:

- The product has an exclusive design or recipe.
  - Secret formula—23 herbs and spices make it specific and impossible to replicate.

o   Coke's mythic origin story has their formula locked in a safe.
- Contains a proprietary active ingredient—ZP-11, gardol, fluoristan, and so on. Even if it is a standard ingredient like stannous fluoride, it can be made to sound proprietary.
- The product contains more of a critical ingredient than a competitor.
- Made with higher quality standards (Six Sigma, organic, kosher, halal, made by elves, etc.)
- The brand has a highly rated track record with independent evaluators.
- The brand is the top-rated product in the category.

There are many more to choose or you can invent support to strengthen your promise, but any support point should relate to a specific quality in your promise.

There should be none of the product attributes we rejected in Chapter 2, attributes like Joy's golden color or yellow squeeze bottle. No WIIFM, no mention.

Don't confuse attributes like popularity as something that should be put in the Promise. Popularity has no direct customer benefit. It can be an assurance, a support point, but not a primary selling point.

The same is true about claims such as "made in this country" or "the business is family owned." These might reinforce quality, but they are weak as promises. Few people are buying the product because of the company's ownership or where the product was made, unless those points can connect to some quality superiority in the Promise such as better ingredients, better growing conditions, or more commitment to quality in manufacturing so there is less risk in purchase.

Don't expect customers to infer these benefits from a mention of origin. Customers must be told why these make the product's promise more credible. National origin can add authenticity to products and can offer leverage for services, like airlines, where they suggest a type or style of service.

As for the "everyone is doing it" claim, or similar ones like "everyone wants one," "number one in sales", let me just say when I was a kid, the times that I told my mom I should stay up late because the other kids were doing it never gained any traction at our house. Popularity is a weak sales point. It might reduce some perceived risk, but it is not motivating, in itself.

Would you buy a product just because of someone who worked on the production line, other than from a charity as an indirect donation? Such a claim might have leverage but only if the overall promise was based on the quality of the work or as a social donation.

Tonality and Character

Like every person, every brand takes on a certain character. Is the brand to be advertised as a fun-loving one, a serious one, sentimental, supportive, industrial, or technically advanced? There are lots of options and they should relate to the category where you compete. Consumers don't want a party animal brand when they are looking for a bank or a prim-and-proper cosmetics brand. Consumers might want a sympathetic or supportive voice for brands that solve personal problems.

Whatever the character, it is best to match the brand's character to the kinds of stereotypes already found in your target's fast brain.

The character or tonality of a brand evolves over time with the cumulation of advertising and other marketing activities. It is important that all advertising developed should be consistent with the brand's character; otherwise, it can cause dissonance with the buyer who looks to branding as a form of assurance, reliability, and consistency. Consumers can start to doubt that they know the brand when it behaves out of character, and they will lose confidence in it.

For some brands, their character can be a critical part of their promise. People use these brands as badges for their own character. Harley Davidson riders, for example, are very loyal to the Harley brand and features such as the product rumble, despite any performance differences (I turned down the opportunity to work on the Harley account because it meant moving to Chicago, but no hard feelings for the brand). The brand has a strong and consistent character and style that is almost more important than its product performance. It is not the only brand like that. Tonality and character should not be overlooked when you are developing your advertising.

The fast brain has been programmed by the slow brain with certain stereotypes, biases, and preferences; it is our way of grouping things to be able to recognize and deal with them quickly. These generalizations about the commonalities of features are the basis of language, and they also include expected profiles of things and people. Sometimes those stereotypes cause trouble when they become inappropriate biases and interfere with fair judgment. They are created socially and personally, sometimes learned, sometimes imagined. But they are there in the fast brain.

Stereotypes come with certain sets of expectations. We are willing to see stereotypes broken but are surprised when they are. Individual anomalies don't always convince us to change our expectations.

The expectations that the fast brain already has should be addressed in the brand character that you wish to project for the product. We started strategy development with "What does the target think now." This is also true of the character and tonality. Our advertising should look and act the part that the target expects or explain why there is a benefit in a difference.

Mood setters such as music can create a context confirming brand character and tonality. So can executional techniques, such as fast cuts, casting choices, and settings. We will review these when we review the elements in executing the strategy, turning the blueprint into a persuasive message.

What Legal or Corporate Requirements Are There?

Some brands have legal constraints on how they express themselves in public media. Make note of these restrictions when you are developing your strategy. These are often required elements that must be in any creative that is developed: logos, slogans, music, and brand usage.

Brands sometimes are required to protect their legal rights to own their name by providing a generic description so a word like "Kleenex" cannot be used by anyone other than the brand owners. Sometimes the lawyers want the copy to also say the word "brand" after the name to be completely clear. I have argued at length that a legal super at the bottom of the screen is less disruptive to normal conversations, and the more the script can sound like a normal conversation, the more credibility it has. Not all lawyers agree; it also varies by the brand. Adding the word "brand" adds some underpinning of "this is a message sent to you by an advertiser" to the message.

In normal life, no one would ever speak about a brand using the term "brand" to describe it. It is not everyday speech and that marks it as being phony. Have you ever heard a friend say: "do you have any Scotch brand tape"? The fast brain hears this and thinks: this is not a friend, it is someone's lawyer speaking, brain! be on your guard.

We had a long legal fight to get the Subway tag line "Eat Fresh" approved. We were finally able to negotiate that it would be approved to use as long as we included a super saying "Prepared Fresh" to clarify what the freshness was about. I found this easy to agree on with the legal authorities because virtually every consumer I spoke with, even 10 years later, had never noticed the little super at the bottom of the TV screen. Cold cuts and cheese are hardly "fresh" in any case. The fast brains watching the commercials were more interested in the action on the screen than in the mouse print (but clearly legible!) supers. Legal intrusions into copy provide negative power to your persuasion.

The creative team developing the advertising needs to know all these legal or corporate requirements before developing the brand's creative message. The same is true about the details of financial offers, drug side effects, and more.

This kind of information requires the slow brain to absorb and understand it, but it is offered in a fast brain environment, a commercial. Effectively transmitting these kinds of complex details is better done in separate communications, better even in one-on-ones, if the desire is really to have the receiver understand the terms and conditions. It is like the argument that my Toyota client proposed.

Consumers need a context to engage their slow brain and pay attention. Kahneman has done studies giving people choices of equivalents such as: would you like a 10 percent chance of getting $1 million or to receive $100,000 now? It is amazing how confusing that can be for the fast brain, even though to an economist they are equivalent. Which one would you choose?

With many legal requirements for financial offers or pharmaceuticals, particularly the side effects, television advertising can distract the fast brain into watching some action, even the verbal advisory that death could be a side effect can seamlessly be mentioned, provided there is something interesting visually to occupy the fast brain.

A famous psychology experiment asked subjects to watch a video of people passing a basketball back and forth among each other. The experiment's subjects were asked to count the number of passes made by people wearing white t-shirts.[2] The subjects did as requested. Few saw that a person dressed in a gorilla suit walked across the screen weaving between the players passing the ball back and forth. The gorilla even stopped and mugged to the camera. However, the viewing subjects were focused on counting the passes and never even noticed the gorilla.

Getting the audience to focus on one thing while something else is happening is the basis for most magician's tricks. It also contributes to auto accidents because we mistakenly convince ourselves that we can multitask. We cannot. Put the cell phone down.

When the legally required pharmaceutical side effects for drugs are being listed, the fast brain is more interested in the visual stimulus of the actors dancing, playing with puppies, or hugging grandchildren. No one sees or hears the gorilla in the room. Nevertheless, the advertiser can rightly claim, per the legal requirements, that the viewer has been duly advised and cautioned about the possible side effects.

The law may be logical, or at least try to be, but the brain is not.

Are there corporate requirements for the advertising to be developed as well? Some companies required "a product of XYZ Corporation" or a copyright or trademark notification to be included. Or perhaps a logo, or some other corporate message.

This is where that requirement fits in the strategy—as a requirement, not as a support for the promise being made. Because commercials and ads have a defined time and space, make sure that these kinds of requirements are clearly included in the briefing before sending the creative team off to develop the creative work.

There may be other mandatory requirements for your ads, such as showing related products, and so on. This is where to note them. The creative strategy is the briefing for creation of the persuasive message.

Now to refresh your memory, here are the elements of the creative strategy:

- What is the current belief about the product?
- Who is the target for the advertising?
- What is the goal of the advertising?
- What does the advertising promise?
- How do you support your promise?
- What is the tonality or character?
- What legal or corporate requirements are there?

Virtually every advertising agency uses a template like this, or a variation of it, as a briefing document before creating advertising. Titles of the sections may change, but the overall paradigms are more or less consistent. It helps to get all members of the development team focused on the same goal and provides the basis for evaluating any work.

You might ask: what if the product changes; what do we do? The answer: change the copy in your advertising, but stick with the strategy unless the change totally negates the promise the strategy is making. This is exceedingly rare.

We were asked to create the advertising for Subway's launch of breakfast, an entirely new product and new day part. At the time, Subway stores were not even open early in the morning so there were considerable operations, menu development, and purchasing/supply work to do to. There was also considerable staff training to do to get the franchisees and their staff on board with the opportunity and be prepared. Franchisees were doubtful if it would be successful.

The marketing logic was based on the fact that the store was already there and being paid for. The incremental cost was only labor for a couple hours, while breakfast opened an opportunity for sales in a whole new day part. There was an operational side benefit in staffing stores earlier in the day to do preparation of ingredients for the highest grossing time of day, lunch.

The overall Subway creative strategy promised healthy food that was fresh.

We followed that existing strategy and developed, among a range of support creative, a television commercial with an uplifting music track. It showed the problems that everyone faces in getting going in the morning, followed by the rewards of a delicious freshly made egg sandwich for breakfast at Subway.

We recommended, but got some corporate push back, that we change the Subway slogan "Eat Fresh" into "Start Fresh" for the campaign to emphasize that breakfast was the starting point of the day. The two words communicated clearly that the commercial was about breakfast and it was from Subway.

Corporate push back was based on concern for changing the long-time, well-established slogan. Would this change be weakening the corporate brand? We got the okay.

We designed in-store and direct-mail materials that carried the Start Fresh slogan as well.

The campaign was very successful and was picked up and run in several countries where similar Subway programs were being launched. We stayed with the brand's creative strategy even though the product was new, and the day part was new. Neither of these changed the overall communication strategy. The overall delivery of healthy, fresh food was the same.

Keep the creative strategy simple and direct. Simple allows the fast brain to hear, understand, and process. When the fast brain has a difficult proposition, it often diverts its judgment to something else that it is more comfortable handling. For example: "I don't think I like this product's idea because the actor's hair looked awful" is an easier judgment to make than unraveling a complicated product promise. Keep the ideas simple for the fast brain to grasp and deal with positively.

How Long Should a Strategy Last?

As shown in the Subway example, a good strategy can be flexible enough to accommodate product changes. Markets are always changing, but once you have identified where your brand should stand and staked out your territory, you should not flip-flop or make major changes to the creative strategy.

Even so, there is always room to adapt, to feature specific offers, product variations, and alternative services under the umbrella of your brand's creative strategy.

True, there can be reasons to change strategy: changes in social attitudes, major changes in lifestyle, changes in technology, changes in population, and other macrosocial changes should be taken into consideration. These are not little temporary changes but large scale and longer term.

There have been changes in lifestyles, family structures, ethnic make-up of populations, and changes in technology. Sea changes like these can change how a product is used or perceived and who is using it.

Products are always changing with improvements and cost-effective changes, as well as delivery system changes—hand soap bars to pumped liquids to body wash, and so on.

A leading heavy-duty clothes detergent I worked with promised superior cleaning. Over many years, the method of washing clothes with the product has changed from hand washing to machine washing, from powder to liquid, and now to capsules. But the end benefit that was promised was the same throughout these changes—cleaner clothes. Delivery of the benefit changed with technology, but the brand's benefit remained the same.

While I was working on the brand, we changed our advertising formats slightly to show the newer alternate washing systems, without changing the campaign structure, the commercial structure, or even the brand's spokesman. All promises led to the same benefit—cleaner clothes.

One major change I have seen is the restructuring of the gender social contract. Back in the Madison Avenue Age, women were almost exclusively homemakers and made the majority of household purchases; men almost exclusively worked at jobs outside the home and never entered a supermarket. There have been massive social changes, accompanied by technological changes. More commonly now, both women and men work at jobs and now work from home using technology. They both make everyday purchases for the household.

As much as the settings and roles have changed, most of the motivators, particularly the psychological motivators, remain the same. We dress differently, we speak differently, we act differently, but our basic needs as craved by our fast brain haven't changed much.

Products and their advertising should evolve their messages to fit their changing audience and its beliefs. Like the detergent or Subway breakfast examples, the end benefit doesn't have to change, just how it is expressed to a changing target. There is no change in strategy but a change in the execution of that strategy when it turns into a persuasive message.

One result of the changing social structure with respect to working and employment has been the rise of convenience as a requirement for many categories. Few people have time to do the things they formerly did themselves back in the Madison Avenue Age. While convenience is great, it is a process and not a result. When I buy a cake now instead of baking one, I still want the cake to be as moist and delicious as moms used to make when they were 1950s housewives. I want the full sensory delivery. Process has changed, but not the end benefits we want from the products.

One product I worked on way back when was Dream Whip, an emulsifier powder that could be turned into a replacement for whipped cream with a little work. Its convenience was supplanted by Cool Whip, an already prepared whipped cream replacement that could be kept in the freezer for easy dispensing when desired.

Our research found that a very high percentage of Dream Whip was being added to cake mixes to create higher cakes for bakers. It was an effect caused by its emulsifier properties that aerated the cake. More air trapped and higher cakes were obtained.

Advertising turned its focus from Dream Whip being a dessert topping to being a secret ingredient that created the high rising, great taste of Dream Cakes. As cake baking declined, the product returned to its creamy whipped topping focus, and then diets changed with people eating fewer fatty toppings. Over time, Dream Whip became almost obsolete. Again, great taste was always the promise the brand exclaimed as it headed slowly off to the Hall of Forgotten products.

Spend the time to make sure that your creative strategy is right. Don't let executional ideas or thoughts for commercials or ads interfere with this process. The written strategy should endure.

This strategy can be used for all forms of communications your brand undertakes: broadcast or print advertising and also its web presence, public relations, event sponsorships, and more. It should influence every piece of output that goes public and even some used internally.

One of the weirder ones I encountered was when we negotiated a hockey sponsorship for Subway and received advertising rights on Zamboni, the machine that resurfaces the ice between periods of the hockey games. We did a repaint of the Zambonis in Subway colors with a giant "Ice Fresh" on the side. That's extending the strategy!

Once there is a creative strategy written and agreed to, it is a good idea to read it out loud before looking at any creative ideas that are submitted for approval. The reread before-hand provides context, and it gets everyone's thinking focused on what they are going to review. When the strategy is fresh in their fast active brain, it provides a current framework for evaluating. A strategy that is top of mind gives the fast brain a cheat sheet on what it is looking for.

If sales are not going well, the priority of elements to reconsider and perhaps change are in this order: the commercials that are running, the campaign idea being featuring, and then perhaps the strategy. But be patient. Commercials, campaigns, and strategies wear out faster within marketing groups than they do with consumers.

Key Elements for Chapter 3: The Elements of a Communication Strategy

- Direct advertising to the capabilities of the fast, operational brain.
- Understand what the prospective customer currently believes.
- Start the argument at that current belief and work to evolve it.

- Determine who is the target audience for the advertising message. It is not always the user of the product.
- Define the goal the advertising is to achieve.
- What is the advertising going to promise to that prospect? What's their WIIFM?
- What supports that promise?
- What is the tonality or character that the advertising should follow?
- What legal or corporate requirements are there?
- Write down the creative strategy. Read it out loud often to keep the focus on what is to be achieved.

CHAPTER 4

The Power of Credibility

"Now wait," I said, "which one is the good guy?"
"The one with the white hat"
"Then the one with the black hat is the bad guy?"
... there is a whole generation in this country that makes its judgments pretty much on that basis.

—John Steinbeck[1]

Being Believed Is Critical to Adding Persuasion to Advertising

It might seem obvious that no message has sticking power if it is not believed. Credibility is king in being persuasive. It adds convincing power to messages. The quote from Steinbeck demonstrates how our fast brain categorizes drawing on visual stimuli for an immediate assessment to decide on who to believe. Once we do, we tend to believe or distrust whatever the fast brain has decided about the source of information, even though we know it is a false generalization.

Credibility is not just a binary quality that makes something either believable or not at all believable. It is a continuum and dependent not only on the source itself but also on the subject matter being dealt with. I may place high credence on my dentist's opinion regarding my teeth; she has her degrees on the wall and her work on me over the years has earned my trust. But her views on fashion or music may seem completely unbelievable. Sources can change their hats from white to black to gray depending on the subject.

You may have noticed that I have dropped little clues into this book so far to enhance my personal credibility. I want you to believe what I write on advertising and show you proof that I might know what I am writing about. These breadcrumbs should show that I am an expert.

We've never met. You have probably never heard of me before. Why would you believe me at all?

To help you believe what I say, I mentioned I worked in advertising on Madison Avenue in New York City. I revealed I did graduate on psychological research into cognitive responses. I have mentioned some national campaigns I worked on with well-known advertisers. There will be more examples.

These are all clues for your fast brain to be able to conclude I am believable when I am speaking about advertising. But nothing about whether I could take out my own appendix.

These references were all designed to create a halo of expertise around myself to provide more authority to what I was presenting. My experiences and desire to share it should also make me trustworthy. These tidbits of information were to separate me from any anonymous person on the street telling you their "expert" opinion about advertising. There is an old saying about opinions… everyone has one… but not all are worth listening to.

You are often left wondering who to believe in an era of "fake news." I dropped those little hints to help you evaluate me as a source of information. I hope they were convincing.

The more believable a source of information is, the more believable and convincing the information that it provides will be. The credibility gives the message more power.

There have been many research studies into the relationship between persuasion and credibility, particularly by the psychologists Carl Hovland and William McGuire. Credibility was proven to give messages more power in creating attitude change. Credibility is the bridge between noticing something and accepting it as being true. This is even more important today with many variations on information and news stories and many conflicting sources.

It is important to understand that the receptor of the message is the one that assigns the credibility to the source of the message. Credibility is not an inherent quality of any source, unlike hat color. Credibility can be assigned broadly or can be specific to some subject area, like my dentist's view on my teeth. And it is temporal, that is, it can change over time. We can all recall someone who was a hero one day and a villain the next day. They didn't just switch hats.

Any source can claim to be credible, but if the receiver does not agree, that source is not credible. This is like understanding a product's benefits. *What the advertiser thinks is not as important as what the target of the message thinks.*

The target's fast brain will immediately assess the source of the information and assign a hypothetical hat color based on its relevant experience. The target's brain will also react immediately to defend its current beliefs. A credible source may open a crack in that defensive armor to get the attitude-changing message through, if the belief and the trust of the source create sufficient dissonance that the subject feels a need to resolve.

So how does the receiver of the message evaluate the source and assign credibility?

Our fast brain assigns this quickly using the framework it knows or is already familiar with, often relying on stereotypes. Rarely does the slow brain interfere to break down why. The slow brain has already provided the framework for the fast brain to operate. This can be challenged and changed, but initial impressions often hold longer than they should. We have all been told first impressions are the most important. That is why.

Credibility of the source of information is based on judgments the operational brain makes on three factors: **expertise, trustworthiness, and motivation**. These are listed in order of their importance.

Let's review what each of those entails.

Expertise

What gives the source of the information their expertise? How do we know it? There are several quick cues consistent with stereotypes that put points on the source's credibility scorecard:

Does the source have credentials in a relevant field? Are they
working in the field the message is about to have hands on
expertise?

Are they a champion competitor in a field relating to the product?

Are they a highly respected person or organization in the field being
discussed?

Is the source an expert in another field that provides an overall halo
to the field in which they are providing their opinion? Is there
data that stands behind the information?

Does the person speak like an expert, perhaps with a little jargon
that suggests more than superficial knowledge?

The judgment is made by cues the receiver's fast brain that assesses
based on some understood logic and mostly style.

A professional athlete, for example, may not have expertise in
nutrition, but we may reasonably expect that they have more than a
passing knowledge as part of their training. Their sporting success is a
halo for what they say about nutrition. That can give them a platform of
expertise. We like to think that a source of information has done their
difficult homework to be able to speak with some authority. This lets the
slow brain rely on someone else's knowledge and not have to make the
effort to do the work itself, some of which it might be capable of doing.

Consider a grease-stained mechanic speaking about car repairs. He is
wearing overalls with his first name, Gus, on his shirt, maybe a smear
of grease on the forehead, an oily rag hanging from his pocket, or
he looks the part enough for us to defer our doubt. The mechanic's
appearance and demeanor give us a cue to their expertise, like a medical
person in a white coat. The strong connotations of medical expertise
mean a white coat is often prohibited in commercials because of its
power to suggest authority. Allied work experience, like the mechanic I
described, can also create an impression of expertise that spills over into
the believability of their message.

More and more in modern society, we have been trained to
relinquish specific knowledge to "experts" as our work and lifestyles
become more complex. We rely on advisers rather than draw on our

logical brain to explain things to us that are too complicated for us to understand. This trains the fast brain into deferring to "experts." It gives experts more power in communication.

The instant breakfast drink, Tang, almost totally owes its success as a brand to its use by NASA in space exploration. We exploited the fact with our advertising. Its portability allowed it to be easily used in space flights and the Vitamin C helped astronauts during their trips. Our advertising never focused on the convenience; the core promise of our advertising was taste, Vitamin C and a share of the glory the astronauts were getting.

When NASA reduced its launches, the brand needed to switch to another expert endorsement. We looked to other scientific spokespeople, mothers with advanced degrees in life sciences such as biology, in hopes of retaining the leading-edge scientific NASA halo. These mothers were certainly experts, but they couldn't bring with them the national pride and sense of destiny that NASA did, particularly to kids. Their commitment to kids might have been stronger but it didn't have the same power or excitement of going to the moon.

There is also a certain expected level of balance and objectivity that comes with expertise. We concede that experts should have looked at a subject and considered its merit with less bias than a normal person. We assume they considered the pros and cons before offering their opinion.

Quality standards can also provide expertise. An endorsement by related organizations, like the American Dental Association for example, are seen as specialized experts. Like NASA.

One can create a certain amount of credibility by comparing product performance to presumed expertise. "Tastes like mom used to make" for example allows the target to create their own standard of excellence, since most people consider their mothers or grandmothers to be expert cooks and bring with that expertise considerable positive emotional overtones.

There is obviously no established standard for "homemade," so from a legal perspective claims of taste "like homemade" are considered "puffery" or simply gratuitous comparisons; however, the target of the message may see the claim as a comparison to the work of an expert.

There are a range of these kinds of puffery claims that suggest expertise but legally mean nothing, because a specific legal standard doesn't exist. Simple ones like "heavy duty," "military strong," or "super duty" (I have seen this on the back of trucks, but what does that even mean?) can suggest a higher level of expertise, reliability and strength went into creating the product.

Expertise can also be gained in casting for ads. We will explore this more when we are converting the strategy into a message. Since the fast brain is loaded with stereotypes, actors who look the part can bring implied expertise without directly addressing it. Curiously, when we switched Tang's advertising from NASA to real mothers with PhDs in biological sciences, some of our women-head-of-household target didn't believe that these women were really scientists. They thought that these women were actresses because some mothers with PhDs were too good looking, not nerdy enough.

That was many years ago and women's roles have changed; nevertheless, the point is that looking the part and sounding the part that is expected by the stereotypes held in the target's fast brain makes the trip to assumed expertise a shorter one. If you look, sound, and act the part, your ability to be accepted by the audience in the part is much greater. Further, the social context defines the role and its expectations. This is also how actors can become typecast.

There are many times when stereotypes are broken, but for advertising, starting with what the target has accepted as a belief is the quickest way to reinforce the expertise that is being claimed.

Trustworthiness

Does the target trust the source of the message? Trusting makes the message more believable. If the source of the information is known, has its behavior been consistent? Does the source have a long record of being honest and dependable? Is the target a member of the same group, collective, tribe, nation, or have obvious commonalities in some way with the audience so the trust can be transferred or inferred?

When our brains were developing into homo sapien brains and maybe before, we lived in small hunter–gatherer groups, tribes, and bands. We often fought for our territory with neighboring tribes. This leads us to trust folks that are more like us, in looks, language, garb, and other indicators. This is a pretty hard-wired bias in our brains. Identifying these markers helps create a sense of collective identity in these tribes—and by tribes, I mean any group that self-identifies as a group, often labeling itself; you might say branding itself. This causes the tribe to defend and trust its members and fear those not marked by familiarity, look, or language of the same tribe.

Our fast brain immediately interprets these tribal markings. The more someone seems to be in my tribe, the more I am likely to trust them, feeling we have a common commitment to survival of our group. It is a deep held belief.

This part of building an identity is the same as building a brand. A brand's trustworthiness can be established over time by looking and acting to expectations. There are subtext messages that can be included in advertising to help build that trust.

In today's world, it may be illogical that someone having the same ethnicity, name (even in part), or affiliation should be more trustworthy than others, but there is an assurance based on the target's personal history that creates a positive halo for the source if such commonalities exist.

In a divided society, starting with a call to "fellow <fill in desired affiliations>" can get quicker levels of trust and therefore credibility. Such affiliations can be religious, political, ethnic origin, and others. It helps if this affiliation is relevant to your story. There is transference of trust to the message from this affiliation—if Republicans think this way, and I identify as a Republican, then I should trust this message and this source. This may be superficial, but it is real, like a hat color.

I have always been fascinated by how supportive and trusting we all are to people (artists, athletes, and movie stars) who have the same first or last name as we do. It is as if it marks them as being in the same tribe as us with shared commonality, shared experiences, and shared beliefs. It is fascinating because it is totally irrational despite what our fast brain interprets with its stereotype filters.

Being known brings some familiarity and confidence to a person or brand that can elevate what they are saying, even if that familiarity has come from another field, like an actor who has always played the hero/heroine in movies or television. The same may not work for the actor who always plays the villain in the black hat. The fast brain does not do a good job separating roles played by actors with their personal behavior.

Two well-known actors I have worked with, Bill Cosby and June Lockhart, were good cases. Cosby has since lost all his luster and trust, but back in the day he was extremely well known, extremely well liked, and seen to relate exceptionally well with kids due to his Fat Albert show and many comedy routines. His TeleVision Quotient (TVQ) scores (a syndicated report that ranked celebrities on surveys of familiarity and popularity) were at or near the top of all celebrities when I worked with him. This was even before the huge success of The Cosby Show, which would have made those TVQ scores even higher.

His personal reputation has now been tarnished beyond repair based on public exposure of his private life. The public felt betrayed having put so much trust in him. There are lessons to be learned by how he gained that tremendous trust and likability as well as how far he fell.

June Lockhart, on the other hand, had played the mom for 200 episodes in the long-running Lassie television show making her an ideal spokesperson for Gravy Train dog food. No one ever asked if she actually owned a dog or even doubted that she did. Her expertise and trustworthiness after being "Lassie's Mom" all that time was all it took. There was complete transference of trustworthiness from the role to the person.

The fast brain uses its known stereotypes to slot the person into what it believes is the correct stereotype and that attracts a whole set of related attributes. Conforming to these expectations is not a truth, just a default convenience.

We can also create and build trust through the use of a "doubter" in our commercials. The doubter reiterates and reinforces the statements made by others, confirming them, showing conversion to the product, being convinced, and making the presenter appear more trustworthy by agreeing with them. The doubter never really doubts; but acts as a pseudo-dialectic voice that sets up questions that can easily be answered. In so answering, the presenter becomes even more trustworthy. This stooge or shill is a common co-conspirator we see on the midway and a regular stock character on infomercials.

There is another dimension to trust that is quite simple for advertisers to create. Does a condition, feature, or product ingredient have a name? If it has a name, it must really be a thing. By itself, a name makes people trust that it does exist and makes it believable.

This is the basis of all branding. For a brand, just having a name can create trust in its consumers. The consumers know what they are getting from it and expect to consistently get it when they see that brand name. This also adds trust to the reality of problems, conditions, situations, and events. If it has a name, it must be real.

From the beginning of branding, the product name created an expectation that had to be delivered. A name was almost a guarantee of quality. It was trust.

Guarantees, warranties, money-back offers, and so on. are other ways of creating more trust in claims or products. While these offers are rarely challenged by dissatisfied purchasers, their mere presence builds trust in the claims that are being made as an expression of the confidence the seller has in the product.

Trustworthiness is determined by the receptor of the message, usually quickly by the fast brain. But it can also be earned. It is based on the receptor's knowledge of attributes associated with the source or projected knowledge based on previous beliefs or associations. Familiarity with the source helps define that level of trust. The higher the level of trust, the more credibility the audience places on the sources of the message.

Motivation

Why the source of the information is motivated to provide it is the third element in determining credibility.

What is the source's motivation for offering the information?

Is the information self-serving for the source or is it altruistic and honest?

The more the source of the information seems to get some benefit themselves, the less believable their message is.

It doesn't matter if the motivating benefit is personal, corporate, or organizational.

This part of credibility is an ongoing problem for all advertising, because advertising is transparently telling consumers a story that is motivated by the advertisers' best interest.

Let me demonstrate how perceived motivation can affect a statement:

I tell you "I am great at understanding how advertising works!" and you may think, "maybe, but I am not sure I believe what he is saying about himself. What's in it for him?"

Obviously, I am promoting myself and have a lot to gain from you thinking I am great.

In another situation, I am not around and someone else tells you: "That Barry, is really great at understanding how the advertising works!" Now, you have more license to believe that it is true and will probably give it a little more credence. You might wonder about the relationship between that person and me and what motivated the person to put the opinion forward. This message has more persuasive power than the previous example.

In yet another example, you are out somewhere, and you overhear some people talking about advertising without them knowing you are listening. One says, "That Barry is great at understanding how advertising works!" They appear to not be motivated for personal gain in saying it. They weren't even saying it for your benefit because they didn't know you were listening. This example makes the statement quite a bit more believable. The undermining effect of an information source motivated for gain has been completely eliminated.

That is the secret to well-acted slice-of-life commercials or testimonials. If there appears to be no clear benefit for the source of the persuasive message, it is more likely to be believed.

Like the other factors, expertise and trust, there are degrees of credibility created by each of the three. It is not an on/off switch.

Overall, motivation is the weakest of the three factors that contribute to credibility and can more easily be seen as negative. If someone is judged to be expert enough and trustworthy enough, you might forgive their motivation in providing their opinions.

Role of the Medium

The medium through which you share the message can have impact on a message's credibility by creating a context for the information. Recall that Marshall McLuhan once said, "The Medium Is the Message."

If the channel of communication (broadcasting, newspapers, social media, podcasts, billboards, online ads, websites, etc.) has some inherent credibility for your target, then it creates a halo of trust for the person getting the information. This is often one of the fast brain biases that arise from media that have a perceived connection to the person getting the information. If someone trusts Fox News, if they trust MSNBC, or a particular website where the ad appears, there is a halo of trust on the advertising. Trust of the source connects well with trust of the message. Another example of a halo effect.

Placing your advertising in news broadcasts adds some heightened attention value as newscasts tend to be more foreground for listeners than regular non-news programming; that is, listeners pay more attention to a news broadcast than they do to a sitcom or music programs. The news might have impact on the audience's survival. Higher attention levels open the fast brain to accept more information.

Our agency once created a one-minute national TV news update to air an hour before the regular nightly news every night for our client, Texaco. The minute included sponsoring billboards, an embedded time-compressed commercial with the regular nightly newscasters providing a 25-second update on the top stories to be covered later.

We tracked positive imagery, trust, and awareness through regular quarterly consumer omnibus surveys for Texaco, and these measures all grew nicely. There were other marketing activities at the same time, but we felt that the embedded commercials in the national news update created greater trust for the brand as part of the context they were in. The advertising, in its media context, almost carried an unspoken endorsement from the leading source of news due to the environment that the commercials were seen in. Some of the trust-based positive imagery likely also came from being reliably on the same show at the same time every day.

Publications or channels that have high levels of viewer and user loyalty generate a high level of trust with their audiences. That trust brings credibility to a message.

A brand can create its own credibility and trust by building its relationships with customers in many ways. Consistency is a key factor to keep in mind, so is familiarity. Keeping the message consistent helps customers feel reinforced that they know the brand.

Credibility is transient; it is assigned by the receptor. It changes depending on both the receptor and the sender. One only has to look at the polarized TV news channels to see different takes on the same events, with each channel's loyal viewers seeing each channel as credible despite the differences.

Ways Credibility Is Created

There are many ways to create a more credible context for a message without changing the creative strategy, just by executing it differently. As a creator of a message, to some degree, the advertiser controls the context, that is the frame of reference for the message. The media context just mentioned is a good example.

The context for the message helps. If the advertising shows you a rustic, slightly dilapidated cabin in a farm country with a hand-written sign offering "Farm Fresh Eggs," you are inclined to believe and buy. It seems like the appropriate message in the appropriate setting according to the stereotypes that your fast brain operates with.

On the other hand, the same rustic cabin with a similar hand-written sign offering "Laser Vasectomies" might not be as inviting. The context changes the credibility of the offer.

Create the most appropriate context for the message to be delivered. Keep the context relevant to the promise that is being made. Remember to think about it from the point of view of the receptor of the message. These will create a more positive environment for the message to be believed by the audience.

I had nothing to do with it, but one favorite campaign that illustrates creating the right context is an early Dannon Yogurt campaign showing old people in the Caucasus mountains eating yogurt. Their ages of 100 and more are superimposed while a travelogue style announcer talks about their longevity, including one 89-year-old who liked Dannon so much he ate two cups, which pleased his mother who enters the screen and pats him on the shoulder. No claims of longevity can be explicitly made, but the context screams out healthy food.

Even small adjustments can enhance the context, build trust and expertise. When she was the wife of a governor or the president, Hillary Clinton was her name. As a secretary of state, she became Hillary Rodham Clinton. Many people experience an expanding name as they become more important or more famous. Adding extra names creates a sense of authority. When your mother was mad and called you by your every given name—you knew the message was important and you better listen.

In the United States, dressing the message in an English accent seems to add some authority to the message, perhaps a remnant of colonial days or perhaps people become experts if they are from more than 50 miles away and a British accent reminds the audience of this.

It can be easy to make something more important by simply giving it a capital letter. It is subtle, but it adds to the importance of a word, like a capital in a title or a proper name. Consider: he sat in the chair versus he sat in The Chair. One chair is important, the other is not.

Names are funny things. By themselves, they can create credibility. Humans love to name things and are obsessed by it. It's the source of all languages. Labeling things gives them a sense of reality that descriptions alone do not. We also feel a sense of mastery when we name things.

Giving a sales event a special name, gives it more importance. For example, "The Blue Friday Sale—because prices this good can only come out of the blue." You can make an event even more important and the opportunity more special and believable by creating a graphic for Blue Friday.

This is a common technique used by TV news programs to elevate a story headline or continuing event. It eliminates the need to repeat a backstory and builds familiarity. The fast brain immediately provides the context. The fast brain sorts things into categories to be able to generalize and not have to reason through everything it sees. The basis for how a supermarket is organized with like products or ideas grouped or categorized together, often given a name. This allows the fast brain to understand context quickly to be able to operate—the cereal section, the canned fruits and vegetables, and so on.

Think of a fashion style: With a name it can represent an era; without one, the style is forgotten.

Naming also creates context for messages. Legislators have discovered this in recent years. No one cares about "Bill-12345Q"; but the "Freedom from Unjust Taxes Bill" can easily gain widespread support. What changed? Just the name. Many of the names for bills are developed more to gain support than to explain what the bill is really about. Your fast brain is not going to read or review the details and feels it doesn't have to get your logical brain involved and do the work if it already knows, thanks to the title.

If you don't believe that a name change makes a difference, ask Bernard Schwartz why he became Tony Curtis. Or consider the efforts that manufacturers make in calling a drink, a "juice," when it only has to require 10 percent juice content to qualify and become miraculously healthy. Every fast brain knows a juice is better for you than a drink.

There is an advantage in naming the active ingredient in your product, or naming a process that you use to create it beyond the generic description. Remember to use a capital letter in the name. Named ingredients add expertise and trust as elements to the product sale. You can always list the ingredients by name in the small print on the side of the label.

Even parity products can carry a halo of exclusivity when they have named components.

Advertising has a magnifying effect on even small differences. I call that effect "the narcissism of small differences." Advertising can make a lot out of a 5 percent difference, or less. The fast brain focuses on that minor difference when it is pointed out, even if it is only a statistically detectable difference and not an easily perceived one. That advertising spotlight differentiates products by magnifying and makes any difference more important through closer examination. The focusing on the differences, no matter how small, also adds more credibility through supposed expertise and attention to detail.

Persuasive arguments can also be made using exceptions as indicators of superiority. Use of exceptions is often understood by the fast brain to be an indicator typical of a population. A single case (what statisticians call $n = 1$) can be held up as an example when it is not really an example but an exception.

For example: "the U.S. education system is the best in the world, just look at Harvard." Or "I drove my Toyota for 500,000 miles. The car's endurance is legendary!"

Most listeners who get these messages will generalize the examples, assuming that they are typical when they are not necessarily indicative of the entire group.

This is like the use of "straw dogs," providing a weak example that products can easily outperform. This creates a sense of expertise and superiority where none may exist. It is a typical technique of politicians against their opponents.

Imagine: "He was the greatest left-handed pitcher to ever come out of Kearney, Nebraska!" which could also indicate he was the only left-handed pitcher who made it to professional baseball and was not very good. Your fast brain doesn't usually delve into the nuances.

On the other hand, you might have a totally true claim that is so contrary to the biases of the consumer's fast brain, and it will have no sales traction. I have mentioned Tang, the powdered breakfast drink.

Tang's flavor was provided from real oranges (as I recall, extracted from the peels of oranges being processed for juice) with the sweetness provided by added sugar. It also had minor clouding agents and Vitamin C added.

We could have claimed that Tang was 99 percent natural, mostly based on the weight of the sugar. Sugar is a refined natural ingredient.

We tested this concept and people scoffed at the claim as being totally unbelievable. Consumer's fast brain thought that the powdered form was not natural, and sugar wasn't considered to be a natural product either. No matter that people understood it came directly from cane sugar.

There were also many who thought coffee wasn't natural because it contained caffeine—which was obviously a chemical. And of course, decaffeinated coffee was even less natural because it was adulterated. Tell me again how the fast brain is logical.

Belief is not what is factually true. It is what your target audience believes to be true. It is not an inherent quality of a person or a message; it is a quality that the audience places on the person or message based on cues that audience gets from that source. The more credible a person or message is judged to be, the more persuasive power the message will have.

To reiterate: Credibility has three main components—expertise, trustworthiness, and motivation.

Expertise speaks to the knowledge or experience of the source of the message, with some suggestions of objectivity.

Trustworthiness speaks to how truthful the source is and has been. The more familiar the source of the message is to the audience, the more trust is granted to the source.

The audience assesses why the information is coming to them. What is the **motivation** for the source of the information in making the statement or claim? The more clearly there is a self-benefit for the source for providing the information, the less likely the message will be believed. The receiver's self-interest may conflict with the self-interest of the source. The receptor considers that.

All these factors are weighed by the fast-thinking part of the brain, sometimes as quickly as in a blink, a glimpse. Any cue will do for the fast brain to designate a hat color—honest or liar. The fast brain measures the sources against its established stable of profiles, its biases, and the stereotypes that it has learned. Then it decides if the source is telling the truth, or at least an acceptable version of the truth.

The more credible the source and its message are judged to be, the more persuasive power the message will have.

Key Elements for Chapter 4: The Power of Credibility

- Credibility makes messages more persuasive.
- Credibility is composed of:
    - expertise,
    - trustworthiness, and
    - the motivation of the source of the information.
- There are steps advertisers can take to present a product more credibly.
- Message credibility can be enhanced through association to credible sources or putting the message in the right context.
- All commercial messages can be perceived to be motivated for self-benefit and therefore less credible.

CHAPTER 5

Putting Persuasion Power Into Effective Messages

Insure the Message Is Provocative, Clear, Understandable, and Memorable

Now that we have a creative strategy, the blueprint for the message, we are ready to execute the blueprint and start building the house. We have a clear path for what we want people to understand about the product and a goal for what the message should accomplish.

This is where the message must be dressed up to maximize performance; the strategy must be translated from marketing strategy into people talk. The message has to be made attractive, persuasive, and compelling to the target that has been identified.

The strategy started with an understanding of what those prospects are currently thinking, who they are, and what promise can have power. What is needed is to translate that blueprint into a message. We have learned ideas about some elements that help make sure the message is believable.

While you may not be ready to take out your own appendix, like Duane can, this chapter helps to understand the process to be able to evaluate the results that you want to get.

A creative team should be hired to prepare this message, the same way you would hire carpenters, electricians, plumbers, and so forth to build the house. How do you choose them? Look for expertise, trustworthiness, and motivation to do a good job. That's right, you need a credible team with experience to create what you need.

The persuasive message doesn't just magically come out of a black box. There are some clear techniques and skills that help formulate that message.

People have been making persuasive messages since before writing was invented. We used stories, songs, poems, and sayings to present persuasive thoughts. Every parable, every fable, every myth, every old ballad has a message beyond the basic narrative. Some of these were advertising morality. Some were to create a definition of a tribe, people, or a nation. Stories explain groups' origins and their destinies with a goal to unify the group. These stories are all about creating a brand for the audience to identify with and virtually all end with their version of an advertising selling idea or slogan.

The constraints of these messages were the medium they were presented in: oral tales told around a campfire, songs sung with predictable rhythms or rhymes, or later written stories. Stories about gods helped create a sense of social cohesion; morality stories were for groups to unite behind and know how to behave. These are a long-form type of advertising using the media available in their day.

Both the stories and the morals of summation are the kind of information the fast brain can track easily and pass on to the slow brain to consolidate. Aesop ended his stories with an end slogan, just like supers in today's commercials: Slow and steady wins the race; a bird in the hand is worth two in the bush; and so on. All the slogans gave useful summaries of the story. Many stories had actions indicated, even the German folk tales collected by the Brothers Grimm had selling ideas.

When someone tells you a fable about a little boy admitting to cutting down a cherry tree, they are really providing you with an ad that tells you that the ideal political leader should be honest and trustworthy, that is, he should be credible. The story is told to enhance the brands of both George Washington and the United States. It is told for the fast brain to follow. It is short; it is advertising; it is a commercial. Is it true? Or apocryphal? It likely doesn't matter to the audience.

How memorable would the story have been if it was only a politician saying, "I cannot tell a lie" or "I am not a crook?" Not very. We hear such claims all too often. That is the difference between what the creative strategy might have been: "politicians are honest" and the final execution that is developed from that strategy, a little story with some characterization and a detail or two (cherry tree, axe). The details give the story more reality; the visual prompts make it easy for the fast brain to imagine as a scene, making it more believable, even if it is apocryphal.

An advertiser may not be looking to change the world or build a nation, only to build a brand and sell some goods or services, but the discipline and structure work the same.

Before anyone develops advertising, they must consider **what media will be used** to share it. Is it to be oral only, or can there be graphics, video, audio, or a live presentation? And what size or length will this message be? These parameters can affect how the message is put together.

The advertising to be developed will be directed at the target's fast brain, their lizard brain, the one that will likely only take a second or two to decide whether the message is worth considering and noting. That fast brain needs a spark to notice the message and a simple narrative to easily follow it. Depending on the media, there are different sparks to use.

The fast brain categorizes things quickly as threats or opportunities. You need to entice the brain to be curious enough to find out more. The initial goal with any advertising is to get the fast brain's attention. It responds best to basic instincts, senses, and curiosity.

After millions of years as hunter–gatherers, we intuitively look for small differences to find things to eat or things to notice so we can flee to be able to survive. A bright red berry on a bush or subtle movement in the woods; these quickly register for us.

The same mechanism operates for ads. Anything that is a little different, even subtly, provokes attention, and alerts the audience. This conflicts with many managers' desires to do whatever their competitors in their category are doing. But it is the differences that attract attention.

Any successful advertising must be noticed by the target, or it won't be remembered or understood, much less incite a buyer into action. The ad needs a lure to attract the fish.

The psychologist William McGuire's model breaks down the process of persuasion into six sequential steps that are: exposure, attention, comprehension, acceptance, retention, and then action. Each step does not naturally follow the other; the audience needs to be motivated to take the next step.

In developing advertising, we assume that our purchase of placement in media of some kind appropriate to the target, or creating a news event, will get the message exposed. We need to attract attention to the message to capitalize on that exposure. That means getting the prospect's fast brain to first notice the ad. We will deal with McGuire's following steps later as we go.

Getting attention is often the most difficult part of putting a commercial together. The opening needs to be provocative, to stand out. The theatrical or visual device used to get this attention should be relevant to what the message is saying or selling. It is not as simple as setting off a fire alarm to get attention.

If the attention is not connected to the core message, it can be a distraction and the product or brand can be forgotten. Back in the day, when a scantily clad woman would attract attention for products such as auto parts, little or no effort was made to connect the woman's parts with the auto parts. Sure, the target in those days was all male, but there was an opportunity lost to convince the audience of the value of the products and the brand. Buyers would recall the woman, but not the brand of auto parts. Some ads became pin-ups on garage walls, which might have meant more exposure, but the selling idea for the products was as flimsy as the woman's outfit.

While getting attention is important, so are comprehension, acceptance, and retention, which are needed to get the prospect into action.

There are elements that should be included in any advertising ideas. When looking at proposed executions of the creative strategy, here is a check✓list: some guidelines for what effective advertising should achieve as an idea on paper before it is produced:

1. **Brand ID**—Clearly identify the brand. If the buyer doesn't know who the message is from, don't expect them to look for

it to become buyers. They are not going to do the work to figure out what you are trying to say. They would just as soon move on to something else rather than consult their slow brain for help in figuring your message out. Expecting that an end title, or a single subtle reference will carry the day is wishful thinking. On the other hand, peppering a commercial with six or seven mentions creates a weakness in credibility by reminding the fast brain to be cautious, because this is a motivated message trying to take advantage of it. We once had a client who insisted on making sure there were five mentions of the brand in a 30-second commercial. She grew out of this quantitative way of looking for branding when she realized that it is the overall quality and clarity of the brand mentions, not the number. Some advocate for a brand mention in the first 5 seconds or so of a 30-second commercial. That is okay, but not entirely necessary if the brand is clearly well identified. Use of uncommon words required by lawyers, such as "brand" or clunky generic descriptions, are also reminders that the commercial is a motivated message. Phrases such as "Well, Bob, it is the fastest selling, midsize, full cargo bed, four-wheel drive utility vehicle on the market…" are not people's words. These are lawyer/legal words or manufacturer's words. They undermine the persuasiveness and lose the brand identification. Think about how you would react if you were talking with a friend or talking to a lawyer. Your fast brain's guard goes up with the lawyer—"Danger! Protect yourself! Be careful what you say!" Supers or footnotes should handle the lawyers' requirements less intrusively. Weak branding in a commercial can result in the viewers believing that any commercial they saw in a particular category came from the category leader, whether the ad was for that brand or not. The category leader is the default assumption as previously mentioned. The fast brain is leaky and jumps to conclusions, or sometimes confusions, and associates any message with the most likely suspect. We see it frequently in surveys where slogans get misapplied to the wrong brands.

2. **Provocative**—If the advertising is not noticed, there will be no buyer response. Ads must provoke to get the attention of the potential buyer. Attention can be gained through many theatrical techniques, but these should all be related to your product, your selling idea, or the setting of the commercial and not be gratuitously used. We make fun of dogs that can be distracted with "Squirrel!" but, really, how different are we? A shiny object, a bright color, a sound, or a sudden movement get our attention. Sound effects at the opening of a commercial, for example, communicate the setting of the commercial and also attract attention because the sound would not otherwise be heard; it is like the bright red berry on a bush. Television or radio can sometimes just be background noise in a room or a car. We want the commercial to be in the *fore*ground with the fast brain paying attention, so the message can get through to the slow brain and get integrated into the brain's view of the world. That requires provoking the viewer.

3. **Clarity**—The message must be easily understood in an instant for full comprehension. We are dealing with the impatient fast brain in a busy distracting world. Don't confuse it. If the prospect doesn't quickly understand, how are they going to be motivated into action. The audience has little invested in any advertising message and can impatiently look away without any sense of loss. Don't assume understanding. Many times, marketers' internal talk seeps into the advertising, terms that people outside the industry don't understand; this includes acronyms such as OAC, jargons such as BOGOs, and others. One problem with acronyms is that the letters can stand for other words. Marketers' extreme fondness for jargon can easily create confusion outside of the circle of those who are using the jargon or acronyms every day.
Ads should not require a "-splain me, Lucy" or presume too much and thereby lose clarity. That includes making sure that offers are clearly worded to avoid customer or cashier confusion and dissatisfaction. Remember who the target is and tailor the

message to them in their voice for clarity. Their fast brain may not respond well to intellectual appeals or complicated ideas; too clever can easily become too cryptic. The language you use should be consistent with the buyer's language: talk the way they talk about what your product does for them. Don't talk down to them or try to impress with fancy language. These isolate your message and lead to avoidance or rejection of it. While working with Texaco, a larger competitor launched a campaign announcing their gasoline had improvements and was now the "No Trouble Gasoline." They spent a lot of money on it. Our client didn't have the same budget available or an improvement to announce. We had a brilliant writer, Mike Hart, who thought that absence of a negative isn't clearly a positive. (You need to engage your slow brain to understand that double negative.) Mike came up with a countercampaign calling Texaco's product "Clean Gasoline" saying, "…always has been." It was simpler and more direct. We had a fraction of the money to spend; nevertheless, our surveys showed that the gasolines were still comparable, and some felt that Texaco might be better. I am not just asserting this, we tracked it with surveys.

Relate to the prospect as a trusted peer or an objective expert in advertising or they will see the advertiser as an outsider motivated to gain something for themself. So, make sure the message is clear. This is another test of projective empathy, seeing the message from the eyes of the audience without your own bias or wishful thinking.

4. **Memorable**—If the buyer doesn't recall the message, they are not going to respond to it. There must be retention of the selling idea. Making advertising memorable is a tough job. There are many techniques used to make recalling the message easier for that fast brain. Some we have mentioned include rhymes, songs, music or sound effects, repetitive words, parallel constructions, and even rhythmic sounding phrases. The iambic pentameter Shakespeare used was to make his lines easier to remember for the actors in his plays. A slogan such as "takes a licking and

keeps on ticking" is memorable for its meter, repetitiveness, and rhyme.

Putting a twist on an older saying makes an advertising message easier to recall, as does a familiar story with an unexpected ending. The fast brain already knew part of the idea; there was less to remember if the idea was built on the known. One useful technique is repetition, as mentioned in Brand ID—but it bears repeating (no joke this time) because repeating helps with memory. Saying the same thing over and over makes it more ingrained and adds some small amount of credibility each time. While it is bad style, generally, in writing to be repetitive, it is not in a commercial. Repeated key phrases start to be sticky for the fast brain.

5. **Uniqueness**—Don't make advertising look or sound like someone else's unless you are clearly and consciously mocking that competitor. The leaky consumer brain will merge the messages together and not recall the message, or it may think that the message was from a competitive source. Just because a competitor is saying something, no advertiser needs to respond with similar language or a similar format. Don't let a competitor drive your bus. Imitation is viewed as a weakness caused by lack of ability for originality. Me-too advertising implies me-too products.

6. **Cost** of producing ideas—Let's get practical. Make sure any creative team keeps in mind that whatever their advertising ideas are, that they must be affordable and commensurate with the overall advertising budget. Sure, a commercial shot live from the moon would get noticed and a lot of press, but can you afford the production or the production crew's transportation costs or per diems up there? As a guide, budgeting 10 percent of your total advertising spending on producing the creative is not unreasonable and is a good starting point. If there is a four-week promotional commercial still use the 10 percent guideline; you don't want to spend the same on production as you would for a brand ad that will last for a year or more. Consider whether

the quality of the production required to successfully execute
the commercial idea is affordable. Many commercials don't work
because the talent or the production time required were not
budgeted for, leaving the commercial not believable. Bad acting
and cheap production can undermine the persuasion power. A
small budget doesn't mean you should give up. Knowing the
limited budget before the idea is being developed can inspire
good creative teams to problem solve and find ways to work
with the budget they have. We worked with a regional natural
gas utility client who wanted to provide incentives for customers to install natural gas fireplaces. They had almost no production budget to achieve this. Our low-cost commercial solution
was a static shot of someone sitting in front of a natural gas
fireplace. Off screen we could hear an argument between a man
and woman, complaining that the fireplace was so comfortable
that their visitor would never want to leave. The visitor is then
revealed to be Santa Claus as the woman remarks "He could at
least get his reindeer off the roof."
We shot the commercial in the showroom of a store that sold
gas fireplaces. It was done in half a day with few camera set-ups.
To save more, I even acted as the male voice-over (apparently,
I work cheap). The commercial worked well and was used for
several years, even though the original production budget had
been tiny. It was the idea that sold the product, not a lot of
production expenses. Throwing money at a problem doesn't solve
it.
The commercial was designed from the beginning to meet the
very limited budget. There are many examples of this kind
of ingenuity in developing advertising, but they all start with
knowing the production budget beforehand.

There might seem to be a lot of factors to consider, but I did warn
you that the part under the iceberg was more complex than you could
see or expect from looking at the shiny part above the water.

Make a cheat sheet, a check✓list, of any ideas that are being considered, to ensure that they meet these criteria. Avoid finding an executional idea and getting swept away with it, forgetting that it may not be the best because it fails on some of these counts, or that a little revision can bring an interesting idea into becoming an effective one.

One overall consideration to focus on is the "net impression" of your advertising. That is, what did the viewer understand in one simple sentence. Remember, the fast brain must feel that whatever is in the message aligns into its currently accepted view of the world and the fast brain isn't big on details.

What kind of ideas work best to dress up the advertising message to make it fit these criteria? Simple, interesting, and clear ones.

A good way to start on developing a commercial campaign concept is to think of a metaphor for the product's use and appreciation. Or an analogy. Or a hyperbole that exaggerates the product benefit or creates a challenging need for the product. What does the product and its use parallel in another situation. It can be real or a fantasy.

So many of the stories that stick with the fast brain start as a metaphor. Metaphoric stories are already using symbols to suggest other activities, they are creating associations for the fast brain to become entangled in. The fast brain can relate these themes easily, based on past references. Metaphors are an indirect way of addressing the product that is being promoted and can use established ideas that the fast brain may be familiar with, so is likely to agree to without much resistance.

We can all imagine a little Georgie Washington cutting down a cherry tree and then admitting to it. A little kid getting into mischief is not an uncommon idea. The admission is a twist to the usual story. The story is a metaphor for honest behavior that can easily be visualized by the fast brain. We love to create little movies in our audience's minds.

There is an old cliché about ideas coming when you are in the shower. Anytime you free your mind to wander, in the shower, or while exercising, or even while sleeping, the slow brain can start making connections that the fast brain's governing framework won't allow when it is busy doing something requiring its attention. When that fast brain's alert system is otherwise occupied or on auto pilot, it gives you a chance to connect disparate ideas and come up with new ones. Sometimes these ideas are useless, but sometimes they can connect your thinking between more than one issue in interesting and useful ways.

Some Italian took some Chinese or Arabic noodles brought back by Marco Polo and added some tomatoes brought back from Mexico in the Americas and created a dish for everyone to love. Our brain's desire to categorize would have separated Chinese and Mexican into two silos, but the new connection became magical. Two familiar, but disparate things, brought together with an idea became an entirely new thing.

Associations between differently siloed ideas are fleeting in normal daily operations, because we have trained the fast brain to reject them and focus on the more conventional useful ideas. Our survival has required us to pay attention to daily living needs. Getting distracted can be life threatening whether we are hunting in the jungle or driving in the car.

The creative brain doesn't reject disparate ideas because they are not functional, but plays with these associations to create new ideas like spaghetti. It explores associations, rather than rejects them. The fast brain wants to operate, to get things done. For the fast brain, it is better to dismiss lateral ideas as noise and interference with operations.

When you train the fast brain to be receptive to lateral ideas, it sees a spectrum, not just a ray of light. This makes it difficult at times for "creative people" to be operational. If lateral thinking is too pervasive, it can be like having attention deficit disorder (ADD). It takes some training for the fast brain to create mechanisms to control this and only engage it when needed.

Succumbing to lateral thoughts happens to people on the Internet, because the associations can be quickly explored in a fast brain click without having to engage the logical brain. You wanted to know when a basketball game that you want to see starts on TV. <click> You notice a star player is from Cameroon. <click> hmm, where is Cameroon? <click> The next minute you are learning about the languages spoken around Yaoundé, the capital city of Cameroon. That's the creative brain linking ideas.

The normal operational brain is trained to stop at the team and just find out what time and channel the game is on. That's immediately functional. But who hasn't fallen down these rabbit holes and only realized half an hour later that you still need to know which channel and what time to watch the game. It shows that we all have creative thoughts, but we have mostly been trained to exclude them as distractions in everyday life.

Most of us must focus on what we must do operationally to live our lives: get food, do our job, travel to the store, make dinner, and so on. We can be fully occupied all day without ever having the opportunity to think about Cameroon. It can be distracting to manage the associations, so our brains turn this off.

Advertising creative people have learned to manage some of that association to reflect some of it back to intrigue the audience and help them see the product differently. The audience's fast brain is interested enough, but will quickly turn off if the associations get too far. The audience's fast brain is willing to learn about the player, but not take the trip to Cameroon or explore what languages they speak there.

Advertising ideas that work have to understand this limitation and resist going too far or asking too much of the audience's fast brain. Advertisers want to engage it, but not too much so that it resists any further interest or be distracted by another idea and not recall the product we are promoting.

When we are coming up with commercial ideas, we want to explore associations. We would often inject random thoughts when developing ideas to take us out of a rut and into a new area with new opportunities to find these fast brain triggers.

We might ask: How would Atilla the Hun sell microwave popcorn? What if we set our commercial in the old west with aliens, or travelers from the future explaining the product? These can be funny and might not work, as well, they can stimulate other ideas—ideas we don't just reject immediately. We ask how we could revise and reform one of these ideas within the elements we need to sell and make the advertising work.

As we explore these oddball thoughts, new ones emerge. If not, we throw the idea out. If you haven't rejected a wastebasket full of wrong turns, you haven't really explored. The idea is to disengage the fast brain's discipline that keeps us on the normal "right path" and allow your brain to explore alternatives.

It is helpful to have a creative partner to bounce ideas back and forth with. In that process, two people, humble about their own ideas and open to accepting new ones, make the best kind of partnership. One of my most productive creative partners and I would come out of a ideation meeting between the two of us, unsure which idea was whose or vice versa. It didn't really matter. The starting ideas morphed and evolved to be better as we bounced them back and forth. The ideation process is not about the genesis; it is about an end result that resonates.

So far, we have reviewed how the consumer's fast brain is tuned to basic needs. If you are showing hunger, fear, sexy… the kinds of animalistic urges we all have, you don't need a lot of time. Our fast brains can pick out that ripe red fruit from the others in a flash, a blink, once they have been trained by the logical brain on what to look for.

The advertising target prospect does not have the same vested interest in the advertising as the advertiser does, so they will not put the same effort into understanding what the advertiser wants to say as the advertiser has put into preparing the message. The onus is on the advertiser to communicate.

Keep the message iconic. That's why visually demonstrating the creative strategy's promise by using the product makes the advertising work so well (see "Strategy Visuals" section in Chapter 6). These visual demonstrations are quick and persuasive, believable, provocative, and memorable. The more an ad can deliver demonstrations of the promise in a relatable situation, the more effective the advertising message will be, because the target can empathize how the product will perform in their own situation. Remember, they are there for the WIIFM.

Key Elements for Chapter 5: Putting Persuasion Power Into Effective Messages

- All selling ideas must be expressions of the strategy.
- Understand the parameters of the media where the message will be used.
- The advertising message is the first step in the purchase chain: exposure, attention, comprehension, acceptance, retention, and then action.
- Make sure all advertising messages proposed to you are:
  o Providing clear identity of the brand they are advertising
  o Provocative
  o Clearly understandable
  o Memorable
  o Unique
  o Achievable within your budget
- Good selling messages are based on known ideas: metaphors, analogies, hyperboles, and twists of known phrases or scenarios.
- Advertising ideas can go off track if the audience's fast brain can't follow them.

CHAPTER 6

Formats for Persuasive Ad Messages

Every Message Format Has Strengths and Weaknesses

How should the advertising message be structured to make it more powerful, more persuasive? There are a few proven formats that can be employed. Let's focus on TV commercials, but the techniques that will be reviewed can also be applied to other forms of media. They each have strengths and weaknesses and can variously be applied to different products, depending on the goal the strategy has.

Some of the basic formats are slice-of-life, announcers, spokes-people—celebrity or invented, problem/solutions, testimonials, candid interviews, a series of vignettes, songs, mnemonics, humor, and hybrids of these.

These formats go in and out of style and can get overused at times. They can also be tweaked to look new and different while employing a tried-and-true format. Very often, there are more than one of these formats in a single commercial.

We can't analyze every commercial or sort them tightly into one of these categories, but we can use typical examples to discuss the strengths and weaknesses of different approaches.

Slice-of-Life

The slice-of-life commercial, or what the industry just calls "a slice," is one where the viewer is a third person watching a little playlet of other people dealing with a plot line that relates to the advertised product or its usage. It is like watching a 30-second play or movie. As with most plays, novels, or movies, the viewer is surreptitiously watching what happens, not involved in it. Remember the example in the credibility discussion about overheard conversations being more believable than a first-person declaration, or even second-person ones. The slice is a technique to deliver the less obviously motivated sales pitch, so gaining greater credibility.

If the little drama is quite true to real life, the people look like the viewer, so the viewer can empathize by projecting themselves into the situation; it can be very believable to them. The viewer's simple visualization of their role in situations like this creates strong memories.

People are used to projecting themselves into stories they hear or see. That's what makes stories so universally appealing. It allows the audience to consider what they would do in such situations without having to take the risk of actually being there and dealing with the situation. That's how we learn a lot of our social behavior.

Throughout much of the Madison Avenue Age of advertising, the slice-of-life was the go-to format for commercials. These little playlets taught people how to use and prefer many products in the situations where these products would be used. The commercials magnified small differences that might have gone unnoticed to create consumer brand preferences. This is what I referenced as the "narcissism of small differences" because placing importance on a small difference, meaning-ful or not, can increase its importance out of proportion.

You have seen it many times. Imagine the clichéd ad featuring two housewives in a kitchen from the 1950s or 1960s. They are discussing what food to serve their families for dinner. Because you have seen the situation innumerable times in commercials, your brain is not that interested, because there may be nothing new to learn.

What if we dress the two women in dog costumes to discuss the dog food they are going to serve. It is now interesting and silly enough to be provocative. We aired that exact campaign for Gravy Train in the 1970s. It got noticed and recalled very well. But it was not as convincing to the viewers as it could have been, because people in dog costumes saying the food tasted great was not as believable as seeing a real dog wolfing down their food. (As an aside, to get dogs to enthusiastically dive down into their foot on cue for a commercial, we would often put garlic paste at the bottom of the bowl. The dogs loved it and would stick their noses deep into the bowl to get close to the smell.)

The message here is that a simple slice-of-life format can be varied infinitely to make it more interesting, more provocative, and more memorable. Creating an interesting variation is a challenge for the creative team to come up with. The format structure works well at explaining the strategy, demonstrating the product, and showing someone convinced and converted.

We started developing the creative strategy with what the target already thinks. Starting the development of the ad creative can play off what is already familiar to make the idea easier for the target to understand and relate to. There is a learning curve to everything new that starts with viewer orientation—"what is this about?" and slowly ramps up to understanding.

Starting with a familiar format can give the audience a quick understanding to let them leap up their learning curve. The viewer doesn't have to start by being disoriented and then figure out what the situation is, what the brand is. It is easier for the viewer to reorient their thoughts around what they have seen before, than to figure it out themselves from the beginning. The fast operational brain has a collection of scenarios to compare anything new to it.

The cliched slice-of-life often has two actors, one knowledgeable and one an unknowing stooge or foil. We see the product in use in a familiar location. The stooge is amazed at the performance of the product and voices weak arguments against the lead actor's explanation.

As to how believable this dialogue is to the viewer rests on the writer's skills at dialogue and the acting skills of the players. The more it seems like an overhead conversation, the more believable the scenario is. The less the listener is reminded that the message is motivated to convince them to buy or do something, the less their fast brain will react to defend and fight against accepting the information in the message.

The slice-of-life format often follows a problem/solution structure. That is, a problem is presented in the little play where the product becomes key to the solution. This is only one of the many ways the "product as a hero" stories can unfold.

We did a very successful campaign for Camay bar soap, which increased brand share dramatically in an otherwise not so exciting category. The commercial featured a woman hero who was taking a bath while enticing her husband to "wash my back." As he is doing this, he asks her what the secret is to her soft skin. She never reveals to him that the secret is the very Camay he has in his hand.

This was a very difficult commercial for Procter & Gamble (P&G) management to approve because it suggested some intimacy that made the Midwestern advertising manager rather uncomfortable. It took months for us to gain approval. Nevertheless, the commercial was a pure slice-of-life. It was a problem solution. There was no dialogue to convince an unknowing foil; the viewer was in the know because of a product explanation before the husband asks. It gave the woman in the bath, and the women who were viewing, power over the man. In addition, the product was the hero delivering soft, caressable skin due to its cold cream ingredient. We love those end-end benefits.

It was also a brilliant demonstration of product effectiveness built into the story without seeming forced. If you can create that kind of structure, it is a very believable slice-of-life.

On the negative side from an advertiser's point of view, the slice-of-life often requires more costly production, good acting, and dialogue writing that is natural and convincing. These are all required to make the slice believable and seem to be realistic.

Announcers Are Not the Voice of God

Many advertisers use an announcer, either off camera or on, to outline the product's proposition to the potential buyer. To most advertising professionals, this is a lazy option because it does not give the commercial an empathetic context. With an announcer alone, there is little intrigue, nothing provocative about hearing the resonance of an announcer's voice asking you to buy a product. It is not the disembodied voice of God coming from the heavens directing you to wander for 40 years. You have to already be a deep believer to accept that kind of direction. Most people aren't.

The announcer is usually simply a surrogate means to reading the creative strategy; asking the viewer to buy the product... and buy it now. It is what every client wants to hear because it is so direct. It is just that it is not persuasive or inviting to the potential customer's fast brain.

When we are thinking of fast brain function, graphic understanding comes quicker than words. Music or mnemonics help recall; they are the hooks. Straight words from an announcer are an easy last resort and probably the cheapest type of commercial to produce unless you have to pay for a specially known voice or person to say them.

There are a few options that are used with this announcer approach: let's classify them as the hired voice of God announcer, aggressive barkers, celebrities, invented spokespeople, and actual product users.

The first format, hired voice, does not rely on putting the announcer into a product usage situation; the announcer just tells you what the advertisers want you to hear. A straight up sales pitch. If the announcer/ spokesperson is not engaging, personally, this is a weak executional option whether they are on camera or a disembodied voice coming from the heavens.

Think of all the times your wife, husband, mother, father, mother-in-law, or teacher told you to do something and how initially willing you were to do it. Unless you already had strong empathy (which for the first few of those you should have) or were actively looking for advice, your attention level and interest was very low when they made the request. The same is true when a commercial is an announcer asking you to buy. And you won't have to answer to that announcer tomorrow when they might ask again.

When some disembodied voice clearly representing the advertiser tells you to buy their product, all kinds of defense mechanisms pop up in your fast brain. It is a difficult selling approach for advertisers. It doesn't always fail, but it doesn't start from a powerful place.

The voice of God is not talking to you, even though the announcer may have a strong baritone and enunciate very well. A lot of the announcers get their starts reading the news and they learn to speak in that deep chested way. The voice that tells you, authoritatively, that there is an earthquake in Peru is not the same voice you want to be telling you that a paper towel is more absorbent because it is quilted. When the station uses their own announcers to voice a commercial for you, that is the kind of authoritative voice you are going to get.

Casting is important. Voice actors are very different from announcers. Announcers have a serious tone; voice actors can be anything that you want them to be, from Bart Simpson to Mickey Mouse to Uncle Jeb. If given the choice, voice actors connect better with audiences.

There are two positive aspects about opting for the voice-over commercial—cost (it is cheap) and languages. A voice-over (off camera) can easily be changed into the language of your choice with very little production cost, just a rerecord. When you know about flexibility, it is easy to spot the European commercials imported for use in North America either online or in media: lots of people doing a contrived stunt that requires little or no voices talking on camera. A favorite has been a seemingly random flash mob that assembles in public to perform a song or dance. The selling can be done with a voice-over in the language of the target, accompanied by gestures and product placement. It is a compromise to multicultural needs.

The need for alternate languages has not been a significant issue in North American markets where the media environment has been dominated by English. There has been rapid growth of immigration, particularly in the Spanish-speaking market in the United States, which has almost doubled from 2000 to 2022. It is now more than 60 million speakers. Who can ignore markets of that size?

Spanish, particularly, is a demographic that should be addressed by any marketer looking for sales volume. There has been, with this growth, an increase in cable channels in Spanish in many geographic areas as well, not just in the southern areas of the United States. Today, the United States is the second largest Spanish-speaking market in the world, after only Mexico and ahead of Colombia and Spain. This is not a market to be ignored.

A voice-over commercial can allow the voice to be restriped (replaced) into Spanish at very little cost allowing the advertiser to reach many more potential buyers. Marketers want to fish where the fish are;

geographically or linguistically, marketers don't really care. The goal is sales volume.

Some seem to believe that if the announcer is amped up, shouting aggressively like a midway **barker**, that the seeming excitement of the announcer will transfer to excitement in the viewer. Let me again refer to your mother. Did it work when she yelled at you? Perhaps, if she stood looming over you while she gave you instructions or referred to you by your first and middle names (to remind you of your connection and her power), it might; but the advertising announcer is gone in 30 seconds. You have little-or-no relationship with them; the announcer can't send you to your room, suspend your screen time or hold back your allowance.

There seems to be a misconception when using this barker technique that the more information is shouted, the stronger the message will be. A sense of urgency carried by shouting does get the fast brain's attention. It triggers fear and safety mechanisms. Our brain must decide whether to fight, flee, or ignore. None of these is conducive to being persuaded. The fight impulse has you mount defensive arguments and the others have you looking to get away or stop paying attention.

Why is it so commonly used? Two reasons: first, it is cheap and second it is easy. But it is not better. Like water always runs in the path of least resistance, advertisers like to take the path of least resistance as well. Again, convenience is not a strong persuasive option.

Relying on an authoritative announcer to tell your story is a lazy solution, devoid of invention. Potential customers are more likely to tune the message out than be motivated by it.

To soften the opposition to the announcer, a **celebrity** or known person can be used. The familiarity the audience has with the celebrity reduces fear and increases trust. The celebrity can create a more empathetic connection the more they are familiar to the viewer. They may not have expertise, but they have a certain amount of trust generated by their past association and they often carry a halo created in whatever enterprise they undertook that made them known to the viewer—acting, sports, business, movies, television, and so on.

It is difficult for the fast brain to think through that an actor, for example, is just acting and not actually being the role they have played as the president of the big company or the mother of Lassie. These associations are already so established in the framework the fast brain is using that to untangle role and reality requires the slow brain to intercede and correct. That takes some effort, and usually we will just accept it rather than make the effort.

Celebrities come in halfway up the target's learning curve. The audience is aware of them, has various associations with them, and imbues them with certain characteristics. Because the celebrity is known, there is a certain amount of trust from familiarity assigned to them. From the celebrity's own point of view, these qualities are assets that can be translated into money paid by an advertiser. The celebrities are bringing with them some mass loyalty and some halo of trust, but maybe some liability as well.

The celebrity should have the right fit with the product and the product's target. Celebrities require careful script writing to make sure that the advertising copy maintains the character the advertiser is paying for. That means managing the vocabulary, the cadence, and the rhythm that is associated with their public self. With some celebrities, particularly sports figures, having them do something physical instead of speaking may be a better option. Their strength is not usually speaking or acting.

They are hired hands, often with huge egos to manage. Advertisers should not turn into "fanboys" or "fangirls" and forget that the celebrity is just your paid-for borrowed equity in the form of a person, which should add leverage to the elements in your product sell. The celebrity (or their people) should also push back if they feel uncomfortable with what you are asking the celebrity to do or say. They have their own equity to protect so there may be need to compromise. Make sure that hired celebrities have a draft script when you are contracting their services.

Social media "personalities" or "influencers" have leveraged "followers" into their financial benefit. Nothing should be surprising here. It is the same model as other mass media has used for a long time:

provide attractive content for free or at a low cost and sell the attention/eyeballs of those viewing the content. How "loyal" the followers are is a good question since many "likes" and "follows" in social media can be unintentional or robots. Research, do your homework using an independent source to make sure that the influencer is the real thing.

As a person who has worked with both Bill Cosby and Jared the Subway guy, I can reiterate that there can be serious downsides to any celebrity relationship. Even if you do your homework, the celebrity can evolve over time from an asset to an albatross. The halo that they brought to the brand can later become a negative association that may take time to go away.

One other issue that comes with celebrities is what we call the "video vampire." The celebrity may suck all the attention away from the product being advertised leaving the target entertained by the celebrity and forgetting what the product being promoted was. The target may be more familiar with the celebrity than with the product. One of the celebrity's functions is to have their favorable awareness transfer in the leaky brain and rub off on to the product. This takes some clever construction in your creative execution to ensure that the brand and the product are the key takeaways from the commercial exposure. Clever message management is required because the fast brain only has so much attention it can provide to advertising.

We were hired to work with Molson, the large Canadian beer company, to create a series of promotional commercials featuring, one at a time, the rock stars: Def Leppard, Lenny Kravitz, Lynyrd Skynyrd, and Alannah Myles. It was for a limited access private "cabin party" over weekends one summer. Folks had to enter a contest to gain admission to the events that took place in remote vacation areas. Only about 500 winners were to be selected to attend each of these cabin party private concerts.

The stars could easily have overwhelmed the brand leaving people excited for, say, Def Leppard (who were very hot at the time) and forgetting which beer brand was sponsoring the promotion. We understood the power of the appeal of these rock stars. To fight that distraction, we wrote the copy in the same style as the brand's regular advertising, droll and understated, and ended each commercial with a specially designed and fully built outdoor deck, in the shape of a guitar, of the Molson logo more than 100-feet-long painted. It was built on the back of a remote cabin in North Carolina, and we shot our closing party scene from a helicopter with people mingling all over the deck. We wanted to make sure the lasting impression was of the brand's logo and the party with as much "WOW" for the brand as the rock stars would bring.

This is what you need to do when you think about your message from the point of view of your target.

Celebrities can be hired; spokespeople can also be invented. The advertising industry has a long history of creating brand spokespeople. They can be people; they can be tigers, honey-bees, green giants, talking animals, battery-run bunnies, all kinds of entities, even leprechauns. Advertising pioneer, Leo Burnett, made his reputation with this idea.

Right now, the insurance industry seems to favor this executional tactic with created **continuing character spokespeople**. We could include the GEICO gecko, Progressive's Flo, and All State's Mayhem, all have been continuing spokespeople for many years, while competitor Farmers hired a celebrity actor to be their continuing spokesperson.

Creating a brand's own spokesperson can have many benefits, because it is creating a persona that can be molded to your needs without paying a premium for a celebrity. If a long-term association is contemplated, make sure to have a contract with the actor, if there is one, who protects the brand.

Creating a continuing spokesperson requires thinking through the character, much like writing a novel about a fictitious person. We create a back story, a profile, even the reasoning why they are obsessed with the product they are pitching. We try to understand the personality we are creating and how our target would relate to this through its stereotypes before we start casting for actors who could fulfill this role, keeping in mind that our actor might change this profile based on their own dynamics.

This approach requires taking a long-term view of a campaign and where you want to take it. You can't get there by thinking only of doing one commercial to solve a short-term problem.

Hopefully, the created spokesperson can represent the users: look like them, talk like them, and act like them. The easier it is, then, for the target audience to see themselves in that role. If the spokesperson is converting others, looking like the target is less important, but they should be someone the target can relate to within their social circle.

We are very social animals, and we are constantly emulating behaviors we see around us. Someone we can identify with acting in a certain way not only gives us social permission that what we see is acceptable behavior but also becomes mini-role models for us. Then they provide us with confirmation bias after we have purchased the product. After you buy a Toyota, you are astounded by all the similar cars you see on the street. This confirms the wisdom of your purchase to your slow brain and reinforces your choice with your fast brain. It is actually a perception trick. Once your fast brain feels affiliated with a brand, you look for confirmation of that affiliation and see the brand that previously you might never have noticed.

Many local advertisers decide to create their own spokesperson in themselves. They jump right out in front of the camera to pitch their case. As we mentioned in our discussion about credibility and how audiences assess the motivation of the source of the message, this is a weak option unless the advertiser's personality can create a relationship with the audience. Few can and it takes considerable time and development to do so. See our "Five Easy Pieces" section, Piece #6 for more on this.

Here's a curious story about spokesperson campaigns that people may recall. Wendy's scored a huge public success with little old lady, Clara Peller, in the "Where's the Beef" campaign. The commercial was incredibly popular; the "where's the beef" line was even used in a presidential debate. The problem for the brand was in trying to replicate the lightning in the jar of that one commercial. The commercial was only planned to be on the air for one cycle and then be replaced by a completely different commercial for a chicken club sandwich featuring neon flashing lights. Nothing like the little old lady who had captured the public's imagination.

The amazing popularity and public hunger for more of the "where's the beef" commercial meant pressure to produce a follow up. Wendy's National Advertising Program (WNAP) committee put the onus on Dancer Fitzgerald and Sample, their agency, to come up with something to outdo the campaign. The Where's the Beef commercial had become a new normal. I saw some of the attempts at a WNAP meeting I attended, and beating Clara Peller was a very high hurdle to clear. It wasn't going to happen and after some time trying, the agency ended up fired.

WNAP decided to air nationally a local promotional campaign used in Columbus, Ohio, where its headquarters was. It featured founder Dave Thomas. Thomas was avuncular and likable. He soon became the ongoing spokesperson for the brand. His aw-shucks, Midwestern persona was real, and it transferred to the audience as genuine concern for customers. The Dave Thomas campaign ran for years. One spokesperson replaced another.

Establishing a spokesperson takes some time and patience. Some portion of the advertising effort must be dedicated to character development so viewers can feel that they have gotten to know the character and become familiar enough with them to trust them.

Local advertisers sometimes trot out their family, even their kids, to shill for their business. It might be a good tax strategy, getting money to your kids as a business expense, but it looks to the viewers like the company is amateurish and slightly desperate. Whatever is presented in a commercial reflects the judgment of the advertiser. If an advertiser wants to get tax-free money to their kids, have them as extras in the commercial, but don't rely on their acting abilities. The advertisers aren't being fair to their kids or their audience or their business.

The reader should have noticed that we are constantly considering the product and the advertising from the point of view of the audience for what is being communicated.

Our personal opinions have some validity; however, if we are not in the target audience, we have to project ourselves into what we believe the users think. Their perceptions are more important than ours in assessing the communications. Good advertising people are professional empaths.

I am someone who has worked on feminine hygiene products and many other products I have never purchased or used. What I have learned is to try to empathize. Although, if possible, I do try to use the products I work on to be able to understand how they are used and their idiosyncrasies. I have worked at Wendy's on the grill and at the make table, in Pizza Hut out front and in back making pizzas, and in burrito QSRs, to name a few, to understand the operations better and what can be done operationally. Obviously, I fell short on feminine hygiene products.

Even if I don't or can't use the product, I believe it is important to speak with many users to see what their feelings and thoughts are regarding the product experience. It helps to relate to and empathize with the customer, what they go through, what they like and don't like.

Testimonials

A technique for creating an expert to speak on your behalf about your product is to use actual users themselves, either current or prospective. Satisfied users can provide testimonials. These can be written testimonials or voiced. They are very believable as candid hidden camera interviews with people who speak spontaneously like they are not announcers. Average people making the normal grammatical or speaking mistakes are the most credible, because they are considered to be unmotivated and uncontrolled by the advertiser. They are delivering an honest, spontaneous, objective opinion based on their personal expertise using the product.

It checks the boxes: expert (through personal experience), trustworthy, and unmotivated. It is an effective technique, but it usually requires a lot of interviews to get the few that are unique, interesting, and convincing. It is surprising how uninteresting the average person can be on camera because they usually control any excessive animation in public settings; excessive animation is what provokes attention and makes good movies. Looking for good candid testimonials may be more work than paying some professional actor to tell your story, but its a lot more credible.

There is a little deception in this because the advertiser is selecting which testimonial to share. Consumer disbelief is suspended because they see the testimony with their own eyes and that makes it unquestionably believable.

The format for testimonial commercials can cut across several options: it can be a slice-of-life where there is a short story of product conversion, or it can be presented as vignettes. To make these more believable, a more "hidden camera" or documentary style with edits and small mistakes suggest that the footage is real and not slickly contrived. The style and quality of the footage adds realism and trust to the message.

We have used testimonials for many clients: from furniture polish where we got a great interview with a woman in a mall in Denver; to car dealerships where a woman quite unexpectedly said they bought the car because she "looked great" driving it; to laundry detergents that removed unusual stains, and more. If you can find satisfied users with interesting stories, their testimonials can be powerful.

Getting good candid testimonials is like going fishing; you spend a lot of time trying and you are never sure what you are going to get. You can get skunked and get nothing or you can find some gems. You are never sure. More on the random risks in producing commercials in a later chapter.

One thing that absolutely must be done is getting the paperwork done with the testifiers. Make sure that their approval is in a signed release to use their stories. Follow up with them and pay them. While most people are thrilled to be in a commercial, a signed release and accepted payment will protect against anyone later changing their minds.

Many testimonials I have seen on air recently do not work well because of short-cuts in production. Satisfied users/customers in these read their testimonial, usually with the script off camera to give the impression that they are being spontaneous. The stilted reads undermine the authenticity of their endorsements. To be effective, the commercial must sound voluntary and sincere to be credible. Otherwise it is motivated, and so not trustworthy. This is a problem that can be solved with some clever production techniques, which we will discuss later.

Vignettes

The vignette commercial technique uses a series of brief clips (called vignettes) of situations, usually each is a few seconds long. Each will show a problem, an activity, or a product solution to a problem. They can be iterative, that is, the same scene with slight differences or with different people, or simply various scenes with or without the product. More often than not, for a 30-second product commercial, we will use at least three situations so that each is long enough for the viewer to understand what is happening and still have time in the commercial for a selling message at the end. For destination advertising, vignettes of various attractions can be used as additive benefits.

Leaving the relationship to the product until the end can risk losing the thread of the vignettes with the viewers unable to connect common unifying reasons. Showing vignettes of landscapes and waiting until the last second to reveal the commercial as a tourism message runs the risk of not connecting the scenes with the destination.

The idea of vignettes is an excellent technique to show the commonality of a problem or range of product uses. We have used vignettes to show multiple product benefits, multiple product uses, and multiple situations where the product is appropriate. One of my favorites was a commercial I wrote for Equal sweetener that demonstrated the versatility of its use: by a mom to sweeten her coffee at home; by a grandmother to bake cookies with the product; and, finally by an office worker to sweeten her drink in a food service situation using an Equal tablet dispenser.

It wasn't the most glamorous commercial, but it became a favorite because my son got to appear in the background in one of the shots as an extra. He was such a nepo-baby.

We were able to show three packaging options (sachet, jar, and dispenser), three different locations/events, and three different user demographics all in the same 30-second commercial. Great taste was the selling idea in all situations. The strategic goal was to support the distribution of all the packaging formats. When retailers see that the advertiser is spending to support a product, they will be much more willing to stock it and keep it in stock. Advertising creates pull from the consumer.

That is the advantage of using vignettes. Each situation can telegraph quickly who and where the action is. That means choosing easily recognizable situations and settings when you are creating the spot, scenes that the audience's fast brain is familiar with. We don't want to disorient them. There is also a subtext to the message that if many different people are using the product, it is a safe and normal choice for anyone to use. When I say using the product, for example, tourism "use of product" means enjoying the destination in many ways.

This Equal vignette commercial replaced some advertising that had won some prestigious awards, but that award-winning commercial didn't do too much for brand sales.

Our commercial was the opposite. It created some strong sales response but no awards. It was like having great blocking and tackling. It was just one for the Sales Win column, not for the highlight reel. Don't confuse glamor with effectiveness; remember where your cheese is; that the goal of the advertising is what's in the strategy.

The vignette technique can be used with music, because it generally does not require a lot of audio support for the scenes that come and go. With so little time, the iconic scenes should immediately communicate, like a symbol or motif. There needs to be a simplicity so the viewer understands quickly and can then see the commonality between the scenes. Our brains love to group and categorize, as we have mentioned in the previous section about naming.

Seeing the situation orients the viewer from its familiarity, but hopefully not so familiar that it is cliché.

Music can add some positive tonality, some connectivity for the vignettes, or can deliver the sales message though a song.

Songs and Music

So, how about music? Have you ever walked into an elevator, heard a song piped in and come out with an earworm from some old hit song going through your brain, over and over? You didn't want it, now you can't get rid of it. We have an amazing trove of musical memories in our slow brain and all it takes to bring them out is a cue to the fast brain.

Why do we remember them? Music itself is a mnemonic device (a word from Greek that means memory aid). The repetition of popular songs helps embed them in our memory. From drums around the campfire to our phone's ear buds, music has been played for most of human history in theaters, on radio, on TV, and in movies to keep our interest or set a mood.

Music videos may seem like a good format for a commercial, but music videos are usually just selling the tune (the product in that case) and not selling us anything except the song and the artists. That's an easy job compared to a product or service.

Music is one of our greatest mnemonic devices. The rhythm and the melody help us remember the words; each note leads into another. Even if we remember the words incorrectly: "José, can you see?" for example. Even without the correct words, your brain has identified the song and can continue singing it from that point.

The sound and rhythm cues bring the message back to us. The rhymes let us know where we need to go next; if one line ends with "above," we are cued that we are likely heading to a line that ends with "love." Sounds and sensory experiences associated with music, tend to live in the fast brain and come to the foreground quickly with a suggestion.

Music also releases feel-good hormones such as serotonin, melatonin, and prolactin to give a positive feeling as a context to the information that we are receiving.

Embedding your message in a hormone-inducing song, even if it is only your brand name and slogan, increases your access to the fast brain and creates familiarity. Like many learned skills, the more you repeat the music the more it sticks and builds a sense of familiarity and trust.

Some musical cadences can be symbolic, conjuring up feelings and recognition. The right kind of da-da-da-dum can symbolize all kinds of emotions and memories.

Songs can be memorable, but messages in songs run the risk of getting lost unless they are simple and repetitive. We might all remember some Beatles or Beyonce or Taylor Swift or whoever's songs, but few of us have ever parsed the words to know what the song was about. That's why we often mishear the lyrics. The song stays in the fast brain for rapid response, but does not get absorbed beyond the superficial. It is rote learning.

One production question comes up: should you use the original hit recording of a familiar piece of music, or do you use something that is similar but different enough to create similar customer responses? The answer is that it depends on the price.

I have done both. To use recorded music the advertiser is obliged to license and pay for the composition, the performance, and the artists. Each of these could have separate owners and require payment for releases to use. A known piece of music comes with emotional baggage, good and bad, that can certainly add to the effectiveness of your advertising. Like the visual demonstrations of product, music is quickly understood without words to untangle.

When we did the Molson commercials featuring rock stars, we used each group's hit music in the commercials. It was a condition of their engagement contract that we were allowed to use their hit music. They also had to be available for our commercial shoot and they were to appear at the private cabin parties that were the prizes. It made sense, if the group was the prize, to remind the audience of their music, which might have been more identifiable than their likenesses.

When we were interested in using "La Bamba" for Pop Secret microwave popcorn, the cost was extremely high for a smaller advertising budget product. Trying to solve this, we discovered that the Ritchie Valens hit song from the 1950s and the Los Lobos song from the late 1980s was based on a public domain, traditional Mexican folk song. Public domain means that the copyright has expired or didn't exist. Public domain material can be freely used by anyone for commercial purposes. This is also true for most classical music.

That meant, for La Bamba, we didn't have to pay any licensing fees unless we used an existing recording. We had our own version of the song recorded with similar, but slightly different, instrumentation and arrangement. This was done for a small fraction of the original asking price to use the hit versions, even the one from the 1950s. If you are thinking of a piece of music, do your research and find out the copyright status.

The lesson is, if you can capture the feeling and familiarity you are looking for without having to pay the high licensing cost for the hit recorded version, go ahead and do it.

Music can create a positive emotional overlay for your message. The fast brain is leaky and when it recalls your brand or message, a positive feeling can be established with music as well as other emotionally triggering content.

Mnemonics

Music promotes remembering. It is not alone. There are many other techniques to help information stand out and be remembered.

If the selling idea is not remembered, it is not going to be acted on. Remember McGuire's paradigm where retention of the idea is pivotal before getting to action. (I am repeating this to help you remember.) Repetition is one of those memory techniques.

There are a range of mnemonic techniques that are available to help your target with retention of your selling idea.

Some techniques that help with information retention, in addition to music, include: creating acronyms, twisting known ideas, rhymes, repetition, repetitive phrases, rhythmic phrases, using sound effects, chunking information, and visualizations that are associated with an idea, simplicity, and repetition. Did I mention repetition?

Acronyms condense ideas for easy access later. Who hasn't learned that Every Good Boy Does Fine (EGBDF) to remember which musical notes are on the lines of the staff? Or HOMES for **H**uron, **O**ntario, **M**ichigan, **E**rie, and **S**uperior for the Great Lakes? All of these use the rapid response of the fast brain to lodge an idea that can quickly be recalled by simplifying it into a mnemonic acronym.

Another technique is to capitalize on an already well-established phrase or saying and change it slightly. In that way, the selling line benefits from the existing familiarity of the original phrase. One word changed can make a difference, or a parallel structure similarly phrased can create easier recognition. It feigns repetition by capitalizing on the known to say something new.

Rhymes use the same technique. When the first word in a rhyme scheme becomes known, the second word plays off the first. Cockney rhyming slang capitalized on this for centuries, many such expressions became part of our language: ding-dong, flip-flop. There is a pattern to these in terms of use of vowel progressions. For example: dong-ding doesn't work, nor does flop-flip. These break expectations for the vowel progression. Like the adjective order mentioned in the introduction, they just sound wrong. So, understand these rules when creating a rhyming slogan or selling idea to allow the line to be more easily recalled.

Understanding these types of strategies is very useful in creating memorable advertising. The highest rated day-after-recall (DAR) score commercial I worked on repeated the same phrase, in two variations, six times in a 30-second commercial. Repetition is one of the keys to learning.

We expect that viewers will have to see a commercial a minimum of three times to really *see* it. This can be aided by creating a high attention context for the commercials, such as the Super Bowl, when viewers are overly conscious of what is being aired. That is one of the reasons why the cost of airing them in high attention shows is so high. Most normally run advertising does not get the benefit of a high attention grabbing program context. It must be provocative enough to gain attention by itself.

Sound effects are a way of punctuating. They can provoke attention at the opening of commercials, they can underline important aspects, phrases, or scenes. They alert the fast brain to pay a higher level of attention. The same kind of alertness trigger that a rustle in the grass created for our hunter–gatherer predecessors. Care should be taken to avoid overuse. Too much rustling can be assumed to be the wind.

Another device that can promote memory of your message is "chunking," which gathers ideas together, like telephone numbers that follow the 3-digit, 3-digit, 4-digit pattern. Our fast brain has a hard time recalling more than three items; remember the research of Miller that from three to seven items can be recalled. That has impact for developing headlines and slogans in advertising. You can use longer lines that work, but chunking them makes them easier to recall. In print ads or outdoor posters, headlines should abide by this as well. Watch where you break the lines in headlines. It matters in comprehension.

Longer lines can be chunked by using a rhyme or repetitive word in the middle of the slogan: "Nothing says lovin' like something from the oven" is significantly more memorable than "nothing shows affection the way fresh baked goods do" because of the internal rhyme and meter of the first line, which chunks the slogan into two clusters with the rhyme prompting the second cluster of the slogan.

The same kind of chunking can be done with repetition to create easy chunks that are easier to recall. The meter and rhyme of the chunks help recall. Words themselves are just chunks of letters that are easier to remember as a group.

Again, short fragments are easier to recall; longer lines work better with chunking, rhyme, and regular meter. If you can predictably group ideas together, they will be easier for your target to recall in chunks than they may be as single ideas. Failing chunking, it is better to stick to the three-to-seven words rule for the whole slogan or headline.

Strategy Visuals

Our capacity for visual retention seems to be greater than for words. Our first writing systems used pictures and symbols before we broke sounds down to letters. Today we see the rise of emojis, and we are succumbing to visual representations over letters again.

Graphics, actions, or signs that symbolize ideas are called semiotics. The visual representation is immediately understood, based on the context. Think of a hand with thumb extended. If the thumb is held up vertically, it could mean that everything is okay. If it is held horizontally, it could mean that you want to hitch a ride. But either way, it doesn't need an explanation. You immediately understand it depending on the culture and the context you see it in.

Think of the meaning a slow dissolve tells you in a movie, or other editing techniques. Music can also be semiotic, communicating complicated ideas with a series of well-chosen sounds. Music goes quickly to the fast brain just like visuals do.

These symbols can represent complex ideas or emotions in a single depiction. Advertisers look for visuals that can represent the creative strategy in a single graphic. That graphic might be as simple as a before and after comparison.

We have already talked about benefit visualizations many times. These are extremely powerful and efficient. They are hard to develop, but once created they are easily memorable for the fast brain and very convincing to prove a point in advertising.

Short common words are seen as a chunk, not a series of letters. Longer words in advertising may require getting the slow brain involved. Needing the slower brain reduces our capacity to immediately remember the details. The viewer must expend energy and, given our human desire to avoid making needless efforts, the viewer will decline to do so and move on.

The audience's capacity for visual recollection becomes a communication goal for all advertising. If they see it, you can sell it. What could be more convincing and memorable than a visual answer to "show me" or "prove it" to make your selling point work.

Visualized benefits are highly memorable. The stretching cheese from the pizza lift shot is not only memorable but also visually evokes what the pizza does for the viewer—satisfies hunger.

Our goal for an advertising headline is to get it down to zero words just using visuals, but still communicate the strategy. Zero words means that there is a compelling visual that completely explains the strategy. These ideas can be immediately recognized, understood, and integrated. No language decoding required. No slow brain to engage.

A graphic demonstration of the strategic promise can be the most important element of a commercial or ad. The demonstration presents an effective way to show performance; by seeing it, viewers believe it because they saw it and that made them feel that they had experienced it.

Not all products lend themselves to a clear demonstration. If you can create one, you can build commercials around the demo simply by creating scenarios for the demo to occur.

We had an amazing lift shot for Pizza Hut showing the cheese stretching off the sides of the slice as it is being lifted up, slowly, from the rest of the pie. (Are you visualizing this in your fast brain right now? I bet you are.) The shot demonstrated the cheesy, ooey-gooey goodness and had great appetite appeal. We used the same lift shot in many commercials for several years. Why not? It delivered the strategy in one eye-popping shot. The fast brain saw hunger being satisfied. It wanted a slice of that action!

The persuasive power of appetite appeal cannot be underrated. It allowed us to spend the rest of the commercial telling customers about other product offerings only available for a limited time or special pricing. We didn't have to remind them of the great taste appeal. That fast brain is really interested in fight, flee, feed, or sex.

Lest you think that creating a strategy visual is easy, let me give you an example of the adversity we sometimes face. Joy dishwashing liquid wanted to demonstrate how Joy got rid of grease, so we took a flat quiche dish as our base because it was all white, wide, and shallow. We put water in it and then some darker grease that floated on the top and was visible because of the white plate below. A drop of Joy created a dispersal. It looked like the grease was fleeing the drop of Joy when it entered the dish.

The production problem that occurred was in making the demonstration believable. The grease had to be dark enough to be seen by the camera, which took a few attempts to get right because shooting translucent liquids is no easy feat. Then the speed of the dispersal had to be quick enough for the segment to fit into the commercial but not so quick to appear unrealistic. This particular demo had to be reshot three separate times. Each time, by a master cameraman, under the supervision of P&G's technical staff to make sure nothing was done out of the ordinary to "fix" the demonstration.

On many food products I have worked with, searching for that "gotta have it!" appetite-provoking shot was like looking for a holy grail.

These shots are not an area to save money in your commercials. You can use them over and over, but they absolutely must look amazingly good with tremendous taste appeal.

We tried for many years with Subway to get an amazing "fresh taste" shot. We shrugged our shoulders and decided to put our emphasis on making the sandwiches look healthy instead. Cold cuts don't glisten with appetite appeal.

Even if the strategic visual is not an exact fit for what the strategy is trying to communicate, it can be seen as powerful, persuasive, and convincing.

We won the assignment of a mayonnaise brand that was not doing well. It was languishing in the fifth place nationally in terms of share and sales. It was a weak and distant competitor. On examining and playing with the product, we noticed that it was a little thicker than the leader. This is a lesson from the homework we explained in Chapter 2.

We explored this with the client. Mayonnaise is an emulsified combination of eggs, oil, and spices, usually with an acid such as vinegar or lemon juice. The category advertising was all about preference for flavor and the distinct taste of the mayonnaise. No competitor was talking about thickness; it seemed an irrelevant attribute of the product. Customers were not looking for thickness; they wanted flavor.

We tested our client's mayonnaise for thickness against the leader. It was definitely thicker. Our idea was to put a spoon in a jar of our client's product next to a spoon in a jar of the leading brand. The spoon in our client's product stayed erect, while the leader's spoon drooped over.

Technically, this was a test of thickness and not flavor. But the demonstration was dramatic. We developed advertising that explained being thicker meant more flavor because the client's mayonnaise had more eggs. In other words, we connected thickness with richness of flavor, even though there was no proof that thickness had anything to do with flavor. Our closing line was "A little thicker; a lot more flavor" backed by visual proof that the mayonnaise was thicker.

Our advertising with the spoon versus spoon graphic demo was strong enough to propel the brand from fifth to second place within a year. The strategic visual showed proof. The fast brain understood that the demonstration showed product superiority. And consumers liked the product.

The fast brain is less logical, a lot quicker, and thinks out arguments less critically than the slower, more logical brain.

With advertising, seldom is the slower, more logical brain engaged to arbitrate the incoming information. The mayonnaise case shows the power of demonstrating a strategy visually. Precise to the strategy or not, it has more power than a claim without graphic proof.

Audiovisual Synchronization

One clear way to make a commercial memorable is to show what you are saying. It gives the viewer two chances at once to understand. A goal would be to have the commercial understood with only the visuals or only the audio. The fast brain is not always paying attention to an interruption from an outsider like an advertiser. One way to ensure clarity of message is to look for audiovisual synchronization. That is, show what you are talking about when you are talking about it. When we see the product, say the product name.

Viewers should also see who is speaking to be clear about what is happening, unless there is a plot element relying on a surprising reveal.

Not being sure what is going on, any lack of clarity, is a great way to lose the attention of the impatient fast brain. If it doesn't follow the story or doesn't understand, it has nothing invested in the message. It has no reason to pay attention or to consider the information that is provided. It shrugs and moves on to the next bit of information bombarding it.

Depth of Meanings

The story of the Joy detergent campaign we mentioned earlier demonstrated using double meanings that can shed a new light on an idea, might we even say a new reflection. That story tells of how Joy cleans to the surface, which allows the dishwasher to see a reflection in a shiny plate. The double meaning of "isn't that a nice reflection on you" puts a new interpretation on the entire commercial.

Multiple interpretations of what is being said in any communication create depth, meta meaning; these evoke new ways of seeing the messages. This richness of meaning is interesting to our fast brains as it looks at interpreting what is being communicated.

Many amusing lines are based on the sudden reveal of an alternate meaning. Here is one of my favorites: "Time flies like an arrow; fruit flies like a banana." It is also a good example of taking a common phrase and giving it a twist as well as the use of a parallel repetitive construction.

The humor is based on a word that you thought was a verb in the first portion of the line becoming a noun in the same word order in the second part of the line and the comparative word "like" has been transformed into a verb. This line is a paraprosdokian, but that's a word for the slow logical brain to file away and almost never use.

The famous Abbott and Costello routine "Who's on First" confuses your fast brain, almost like tickling causes you to laugh. In the routine, we listen to two people talking, seemingly about the same thing, but not really. That kind of multiple meaning engages and fascinates your fast brain as it tries to make sense of the disparity of the meanings.

Any good writer will be looking for multiple connections and levels of meaning. My personal goal is to get to three levels of meaning. If a story can do that, it has more engaging and lasting power. We might get from basketball to team to player, but getting further, all the way to Cameroon is too much of a challenge in 30 seconds.

Multiple levels of meaning are what make stories richer and more interesting. Every fable or parable has a surface narrative that tells a story we can easily relate to, even if it features such nonhumans as a hare and a tortoise. That superficial story should represent more than the obvious. It should not just borrow interest by staging a race between two animals and then reveal a surprise ending. Or, in an abrupt switch, that there is a product, and it has a benefit for you.

The narrative in any advertising should be inexplicably interconnected with the creative strategy and the product in a natural way.

Meta meanings make slogans, end lines, and selling lines much more memorable. There is a danger of being cryptic and not understood, so there should be cues that help the viewer move easily to the strategic conclusion that the line was designed to bring the viewer to.

I know, as a writer, I can sometimes make references that I think are obvious, but others have no idea what I am talking about. Again, projecting and empathizing with the audience's point of view can help avoid turning rich lines into nonsequiturs.

Humor

Self-admission here, I love the use of humor in persuasion. Humor opens the target's brain for awareness, acceptance, and retention by reducing its need for defense.

I also hate the use of jokes.

How do I reconcile these two? Easy.

When I tell someone a joke the first time, they laugh. They might even laugh a little the second time. But their fast brain has now learned the catch, the surprise twist, the play on words that made it funny. The third time, it just isn't funny. Have you heard that "time flies like an arrow; fruit…" oh, you have heard it before.

Humor, on the other hand, brings a smile and a positive feeling to an idea. I mentioned Bill Cosby. He rarely told a joke. He would do an hour of stand-up comedy, and the humor would be in the stories he told and how he told them. The Seinfeld TV show rarely told jokes, other than when Jerry was performing. They would set up a running gag as a theme, but it was usually based on the predicaments that the main characters got involved in. That was the source of the humor. Gags don't wear as well as the situations. The more laugh-out-loud the joke is, the shorter its effective lifetime.

The warm smile coming from a situation brings a bonding to the story; it creates some empathy between the viewer and the story. That is exactly what we are looking for in a commercial—a bonding between the story we are telling about the product and the viewer of that story. We want empathy for the demonstration of the product benefit. The warm smile relaxes the flee or flight reflex of the fast brain—no danger here—and allows us to talk more directly to the logical brain to help convert it to the idea we are promoting.

One factor that makes a huge difference in the use of humor is relevance. If the humor is not relevant to the product or its use, it is what we call "borrowed interest" and more of a distraction than a help in communicating your message. It also suggests that the source of the humor and the message are not in tune with the audience.

Humor can also indicate confidence in the message or product. Who would make fun of themselves or their message unless they were completely confident in it?

Think of the extreme case of a politician who goes to speak at a religious conference and starts by telling a joke about a farmer, a hooker, and an elephant walking into a bar. It might just be considered in bad taste, or more likely and more seriously it would be a strong signal to the audience that the speaker is not trustworthy. Not trustworthy = not credible. Why believe anything further the speaker has to say? Again, the acid test is in taking the audience's point of view on what the message says.

Borrowed interest is the same. Like the video vampire mentioned earlier, it diverts your audience's attention from your selling points, an attention you may not get back.

Relevant humor, on the other hand, shows confidence and helps the fast brain lower its defenses to hear your story. The humor also makes the source seem friendlier and less threatening.

Humor can help, but it must be used judiciously. It is a two-edged sword.

Print Advertising

A lot of what we have discussed about execution of the strategy relates to broadcast advertising. The thinking applies to print ads as well. Let me add a few additional elements that help improve the persuasive power for print, posters, and digital advertising—or any static messages.

- Keep headlines short—unless you are using the length for effect, stick to seven words or less. The goal is to have as few words as possible, even zero. Immediate understanding is the goal.
- Visuals can reduce the need for words. A visual that tells the strategic story encapsulates all you need to say.
- Don't get too clever. Words require decoding time from the fast brain. Recall the higher level of effectiveness for the "Clean Gasoline" ad versus the "No Trouble Gasoline" competitor.
- English has some tough words to immediately understand on sight, so care must be taken in using them. Don't make the fast brain work too hard; it is lazy and won't cooperate.
- A provocative headline and a photo of the product are not engaging enough unless the headline strategically relates clearly to the product benefit.
- Make sure that each line of the headline makes sense. Use line breaks like poets do; don't break thoughts in midline. People read visually in chunks, so make sure each chunk is understandable.
- Use evocative graphics. Without storytelling pictures, you might as well use radio. Pictures have power to suggest a story.
- Proofread your advertising. Relying on spell check won't always fix "they're," "their," or "there." It can undermine your brand's credibility to have the wrong word or a misspelled word in the copy. If the ad is sloppy, the product might be too.

Feature Pricing

Price may be a last resort, but sometimes advertising must go there. The critical thing to remember is how poorly the fast brain does math. As we mentioned, it can do 2 × 2 but nothing complicated. That gave rise to the 99 cents price point that the fast brain consistently sees as being more associated with the number in front of it, than the closer number one cent higher.

The fast brain has a hard time differentiating between correlations and cause and effect; it assumes cause much more often than it should.

Everyone who confuses causation with correlations ends up dying. It is reasonable for a part of the brain entrusted with jumping to the survival conclusions that a tiger might be coming if the grass starts to rustle. Comparing prices can use this lack of logic.

The fast brain also sees the short-term needs for cashflow-based pricing as being more manageable than the longer term costs of goods for things such as vehicles. Advertising that features a cashflow price tells the customer's fast brain how much they will pay each month or week. These show a lower price that appeals to customers more than the total price, although that full price would have to be revealed in the final paperwork.

Cost per week or cost per month are ways the fast brain manages its cashflow based on paychecks deferring longer term, larger capital costs off to the future self. The future self is not there in the here-and-now and can't complain. Many of Kahneman's Thinking Fast and Slow experiments showed that the fast brain looks at short-term and defers the long-term responsibility feeling that in many ways it is hypothetical, not really coming out of this week's paycheck.

The psychologist Walter Mischel did an experiment testing the development of the slow thinking brain's ability to provide self-control for longer term gain.[1] With self-control, a person has a much greater possibility for success in almost all facets of their life. He presented young kids, 3 to 5 years old, with a marshmallow and told them they could eat it or wait 15 minutes and receive a second marshmallow. It was a contest between self-control that comes from the logical brain and the immediate gratification that the fast brain wants. Self-control allows a person to forego immediate gratification and make the longer play for greater rewards. Very few kids could endure looking at the marshmallow and not eating it. Most tried to consciously distract themselves into doing or thinking something else.

This kind of orchestrated self-deceit is performed on many purchases where the larger price impact occurs later. It is also why impulse purchases, especially foods we crave, are driven by the fast brain looking for immediate gratification. We counsel consumers to eat a meal before going to the supermarket to subdue the hunger drive from their fast brain. It is also why those impulse "rewards" are located at the end of shopping when the buyer can envisage immediately eating them.

Anchor pricing can also present a reference point for the fast brain to operate from. Anchor pricing is when a specific reference price is cited as a base for comparisons, in advertising or at point of sale. Comparing a product price with similar products, or as a reduced price on the product itself, gives consumers a reference, but the price differences created by the detailed differences often goes unnoticed or not understood.

Technology that is changing rapidly, for example, leaves many customers not knowing, or maybe even caring, whether they have the latest most expensive tech, or something a half a step behind and at a considerably lower price. Others "gotta have it" if the model is the newest and latest whether there is a demonstrable, noticeable difference or not. The buyer's fast brain assumes, if there is a comparison being made (like model 10 versus model 9) that there is a meaningful difference, such as the volume control in Spinal Tap that goes all the way to 11.

Sale events where an older, higher price is visible create more sales, because the fast brain sees the savings without ever considering whether the original anchor price was a fair one or whether the comparison is a fair one.

Summary

We have gone through some formats, styles, and techniques that are most often used in advertising. Some formats have more inherent persuasive powers than others.

Sometimes clients get so excited about what they have done that they think the whole world is just as excited about it. As a couple of episodes of Shark Tank will tell you, not everyone is ready to immediately jump on board any idea. If you build it, they won't likely come. If you build it, you will wait and wait and hope and hope waiting to be lucky.

Just showing up by doing some advertising is not enough. The advertising must be persuasive to efficiently work.

A well-developed advertising campaign that has the right motivating power, provokes attention, is memorable, clear, and unique.

Advertising spreads the word faster using available media to reach selected people, because they have a greater propensity to be interested in the idea. That is putting rocket fuel on the learning curve. Getting people more quickly aware, understand, and interested in the product, instead of waiting for them to discover it in the haphazard manner that information spreads.

The opportunity lost while a product waits to be discovered can be fatal. The cost of waiting should be balanced against the cost of investing to get faster awareness and trial for the product. The faster the trial happens, the faster you have regular users and a revenue stream.

Of course, there are exceptions that become unicorns overnight. But for every such exception there are hundreds of decent ideas that wallow waiting and eventually give up as their patience and their money run out.

No basketball team has success if their only strategy is waiting for the next 7-foot 5-inch Yao Ming to show up! Extraordinary exceptions are not typical. Nevertheless, never cease from exploration of ideas that might to be great.

Advertisers should constantly be looking for alternate campaigns, having backup ideas ready, and being prepared for unforeseen eventualities. That's just good management.

Key Elements for Chapter 6: Formats for Persuasive Ad Messages

- Demonstrate the product or service in believable situations.
- Advertising message formats often used include:
  - o   Slice-of-life can be very believable.
  - o   Announcers—telling is not persuading.
  - o   Spokespeople—celebrity or invented; their halos help.

- Don't lose attention to the product through a video vampire.
  - Products that serve as solutions to problems are easy to understand.
  - Testimonials, including candid interviews.
  - Vignettes show ranges of users and uses.
  - Songs and music can provide tone and memorability.
  - And many others including hybrids of all these.
- Look for mnemonics (memory aids) to help buyers recall.
- Strategic visuals—graphic demonstrations of the products promise have power.
- Make sure there is audiovisual synchronization in messages.
- Try to achieve depth of meaning for enduring power in the messages.
- Be careful with humor. Smiles are great but jokes wear out.
- Use the kind of language product users use. Assess selling ideas from the point of view of the users.
- Print and digital advertising has additional rules for its elements.
- Pricing claims should use psychological frameworks for the fast brain.

That's a lot of elements to recall. It might be worthwhile to read this page again. Repetition helps memory.

CHAPTER 7

Evaluating Advertising Ideas

A Checklist for Messages Before Producing Them

We will assume that your creative team is developing the creative messages and presenting these ideas to you as the manager. They should bring with them the technical skills needed to make everything fit into the specifications of the ad space, production, time, and budget limitations.

What kind of discipline should be used in responding to the presentation of advertising ideas? How should the work be judged? What do you say and do, as the manager?

There are several questions to ask yourself and to ask those presenting. Before any presentation begins, start by rereading the creative strategy out loud to get everyone's mind set on the same wavelength. This reestablishes the framework in everyone's fast brains and makes sure everyone is speaking the same language. It may sound redundant in mentioning this every time that there are important decisions to be made, but in the creative process, so many new and exciting ideas can emerge, and managers really do need to reinforce the goal and strategy for the work to make sure that they are all still on track and all aiming at the same goal.

Listen carefully to the ideas being presented. Normally, more than one idea is requested for presentation. If so, wait for all options to be presented before making comments to get the full range of thinking. It can be easy in a meeting to get derailed by an exciting element in one idea and not be able to consider others. The fast brain can easily suffer from ADD and lunge for a shiny object instead of being a grown up and considering the options.

Ask for a recommendation on which of the options the team believes is the strongest. Then ask why? What is their thinking on the strengths of one versus another.

Are all options consistent with the written creative strategy?

If an idea is not a clear expression of the creative strategy, stop right there. Go directly to jail; do not pass go; do not collect $200. Toss it out! You need another idea.

If the idea is not on strategy, no matter how interesting it is, it is not worth continuing with it. If there is any doubt about whether it is on strategy, ask the presenters to provide an explanation as to why or how it might be on strategy. If everyone is not convinced, toss it aside or send it back for more work to find a way to get it on strategy.

In assessing the advertising presented, here is a quick check✓list to follow to determine the strength of the selling ideas presented.

- Do you easily understand the message that is being presented?
- Is the selling idea clear and simple?
- Is the brand clearly indicated? How many times is it mentioned?
- What is your quick and immediate response to the idea? Do you like it? Is it interesting? Does it immediately get your attention?
- Is the message memorable? Involving? Believable? Unique?
- Did the opening get your attention right away? Was it a positive message?
- Is the idea extendable? Could it form the basis for a campaign?

Is there audio–video synchronization? That is, does the copy match, on time, with the visuals that the audience will be seeing? Is the idea understandable with only the visuals or with only the audio? Does the story track through?

Would the target the strategy has defined identify with the message? This might be a test of your ability to project empathy with your target; but try to put yourself into the head of your customer. Whether the message is something you, yourself, would respond to is immaterial. The advertising is not aimed at or about you; it is about your customer.

Could you explain this idea in less than 30 seconds? Could it be explained in an "elevator pitch?" That is, in the time an elevator can go up a few floors; assume that the trip usually takes around 30 seconds. When an idea is being presented in a meeting, the presenters normally provide a preamble, setting the stage for the advertising idea. They give you many suggestions and prep you for the idea as groundwork before the idea is revealed. They create a context for seeing the idea.

When the commercial message is shared with the public through any media, there will be no preamble from an agency. The idea must stand on its own in isolation. Does the idea you are considering stand on its own—without a preamble and build up, without an explanation?

Listen carefully to the responses to questions from the creative team. Remember, you did not buy a dog to bark yourself, so don't try to rewrite the concepts or scripts.

Client comments on creative work presented should be phrased as questions that can have open answers. They should be probes. The manager's job is to be the sounding board for the public and to ensure that the strategic requirements have been met, that the advertising achieves what you are looking for it to achieve.

As a manager, you also want to measure the confidence that your creative team has in their recommendation. The probes about the work will give an understanding of how much thought has gone into the work that is being presented.

Ask questions about expected production issues, including costs. About clarity. About brand identification. All the items discussed in Chapter 5 said should be there.

Once an advertising idea has been approved, there are usually subsequent steps to take as well. Getting approval from senior management, for example.

Before production, a script may need approval through a technical review or through a legal department. If it is a television commercial, it may need approval through network standards clearance or other outside organizations.

Each of these steps may result in questions or requested changes. Make those commenting on the advertising, ask questions or challenge claims rather than make copy suggestions. Don't ask them for changes or you will get them and they may not be good.

It is good practice to involve the creative team in addressing these issues or the concept can get chipped away with many "Kilroy was here" kinds of changes. These are small, non-necessary changes that someone requests to leave their personal imprint on the commercial. Most of these are arbitrary and if not made won't improve anything. It is sort of like what animals do to mark their turf, but these changes are not usually positive revisions. From the creative team's point of view, it can undermine their sense of authorship and ownership of their work.

If you are managing the process, you want the best work. This should not mean that there is a competition between the person who approves the work and the writer. You should manage the process from above, not descend into the process. Once you step into the process, it becomes your job ... nobody else's. Writing ad copy to appeal to your audience is not the same as writing business memos or proposals to appeal to the management. You want to keep your creative team feeling ownership and responsibility for the final production, so you should involve them in providing solutions to outside comments such as those from technical or legal sources.

There are many kinds of testing techniques that can be employed to get a better understanding of what the idea is communicating and how compelling the selling idea that is expressed can be. Most of these can be done before the costly production process.

We are not going to review all the creative testing options here. My experience is that quantitative testing is more effective than using qualitative techniques. It is extremely difficult to measure the longer term cumulative impact of advertising.

Most testing assesses immediate responses to ideas that come from the fast brain. They can tell you how provocative your idea is, how easily it can be recalled and, to some degree, how it might be projected into sales. They can tell you if it is likable, if it is clear, if it is consistent with who the subjects feel the brand is.

Testing by floating ideas out through e-mail blasts or social media for responses is not a strong option. It is cheap, for sure. You can see which lures people bite on, but you don't have an understanding why without further probing. It could be a statistical anomaly relating to external variables and you would never know. A slight wording change or the addition of a Johnson box (a box placed above the text of the appeal letter in direct mail that highlights the offer) or some other device that might increase response rates, but that is not a long-term selling idea. They are executional fine-tuning.

Blasting away options also runs the risk of wasting exposures or alienating some potential customers. A little thinking about the content and the strategy is a stronger way to improve the elements in your advertising and make it work better. It requires using the slow brain and not just the fast one.

Qualitative research works best as a resource for providing guidance to how ideas are expressed, learning the language the prospects use and understanding how those prospects integrate the ideas into their lives.

The use of focus groups can be very bad methodology if they are not well structured and controlled. Individuals can dominate. Groups can go off track. Recruiting can be expedient and therefore not representative of your market. You may arrive at a state of GIGO—garbage in and garbage out. You are spending effort; you should want useful results.

Don't draw too much selling idea direction from such group sessions. Don't defer making a business decision by simply abdicating to some test results. Testing can guide you, but it should not make your decisions for you.

One way to assess the creative message is to look backward. Consider the commercial and ask yourself if it achieved the goals that had been set out for it. Is the promise clear? Are the support reasons well connected to that promise? Does the copy connect with the target that was identified? Does the commercial's proposition address the accepted belief that the consumer has?

If your commercial scores on all the goals we have laid out, don't worry too much. It may not be a tape measure home run, and people may think it is bad, but hitting it out of the park is a low percentage play and deferring to people outside the decision-making group is not part of the strategy. Judge it instead on the results that it brings in, on the objective you articulated in the strategy. That's the only opinion that really counts.

Even professionals working in the business are not infallible at being able to judge which campaigns and commercials will endure and be successful and effective.

I have included a story as Chapter 12 in this book about the process and professional marketers and advertising people's inability to predict what will be a successful message.

If the message has checked all the boxes that we have been discussing so far in this book, you have heightened your advertising's odds of success and reduced the risk of wasting your money.

Key Elements for Chapter 7: Evaluating Advertising Messages

- All creative ideas should be consistent with the creative strategy.
- All creative ideas should be clear and easy to understand.
- Is the product or brand clear and integral to the commercial?
- Is the message memorable? Involving? Believable? Unique?
- Did the opening get your attention right away?
- Is there audio–video synchronization?
- Does this show your target in a way that they can identify themselves?
- Does it speak the way they speak?
- Could you explain the entire concept in 30 seconds?
- Can the advertising be produced within your budget?

CHAPTER 8

Advertising Approval Process Challenges

Resist Letting Organizations Wear Ideas Down Before Approval

This chapter is more like a travelogue. The voyage of an advertising message is rarely a nonstop direct flight from creation to on-air or publication. Managing that trip is important in arriving at the point where the message issued is as minimally distorted and as strong as possible. This means avoiding a lot of changes to avoid alleged risk, pasteurizations, and homogenizations that come through the process.

I once wrote a long article for NYU's *Media Ecology Journal* describing the multitude of steps required from when the need for advertising was identified, through the development of a strategy, then for the idea to come forth from some creative team's mind in a large agency. Then I listed the steps that selling idea had to go through to be translated from strategic language into a script or layout for public consumption. The idea travels through the many levels and departments of an agency, meeting after meeting, before it gets to be presented to the agency's clients.

From agency approval, the work then goes through the various levels on up of client organizations, meeting after meeting. After the work has cleared these hurdles, there may be scientific or legal department approvals at the client organization as well, depending on the claims being made.

There were so many steps and possible additional steps that I described in my article, I couldn't count them. Many with twists and turns. This is normal in corporate America. Decisions rarely come quickly.

Advertising ideas almost never spontaneously emerge out of nowhere. Writers and agencies are paid by clients and log hours against projects. Agencies almost never initiate work without knowing it will be billable. Who works for free these days? In any case, if you don't know the strategy and application requirements, coming up with ideas is a waste of time.

Many times, I have been approached by people who claim to have the perfect advertising idea for a client of mine, but these ideas are not related to what we are trying to achieve. They are just someone's fanciful idea for an ad that doesn't connect with the marketing strategy we have. It is dangerous to even listen to these because some idea may come up later that is similar, and we would have the "volunteers" claiming ownership.

The advertising approval process forces decision makers, using their slow logical brain, to evaluate advertising ideas that are to appeal to the target's fast brain that responds to basic needs. Too much logical brain assessment is like writing in Spanish to appeal to people in English. It is difficult for the approver to understand the ad's impact entirely. Projective empathy is not easy; but it is not impossible.

David Ogilvy once made a training video of how his famous print ad for Hathaway Shirts would fare. The famous ad shows a single photo of a very confident man wearing a Hathaway dress shirt looking boldly to camera. He is distinctive because he wears an eye patch. The strategy was to show the shirt as creating an air of confidence for even the most dashing man.

Ogilvy imagines the ad passing through corporate approval levels. In one meeting, there is a request to add inset shots of different shirt styles to show the full Hathaway line. In the next meeting, the ad is revised to show the man at point of purchase in a department store. Then a request is made to add a woman admirer because women were known to make the majority of men's shirt purchases. Finally, there was the question of the eye patch—was the man disabled; did he have an eye infection?

The bold statement had eroded to become a safe and ordinary ad looking like all others in the category. A safe ad that does not appeal to anyone and offends no one. The patch was a semiotic for a daring risky life, not an indication of conjunctivitis. This is what happens when the logical brain meets the interests embraced by the fast brain.

The risks of passing through this approval process bring idea erosion where the provocative and involving idea is worn away, like the removal of the eyepatch.

Sometimes the opposite occurs where an idea is seen within an organization as being exciting, even if it is off strategy. This is organizational groupthink, especially if the idea has a corporate champion with political clout. Someone has to tell the emperor that he has no clothes on. It is difficult in some organizations when the senior decision maker champions an idea that might not fit, but still likes it based on personal "judgment" about it.

To maintain discipline, I would encourage reading the creative strategy before any advertising copy of the decision-making meeting. It reestablishes the framework that should be at the forefront of thinking when making any decisions. It reloads the fast brain about staying on course to allow the slow brain to do the decision making and confirms the direction the group is taking. Reiterating the strategy reminds those making the decision of who is the target of the advertising and what is the promise made to achieve its goal. It is also a good idea to remind those who will be approving creative, that you are looking for approval or questions, not for specific input.

Organizations that streamlined the decision-making process were always much easier to deal with and do great work for as an advertising agency. The streamlining helped avoid the erosion problem. There were fewer suggestions or minor word changes requested.

I enjoyed my relationship with the marketing team at Texaco and was able to present significant, breakthrough creative and media ideas through no more than two levels: marketing department and the CEO of the company. It took us a year or so to earn that expedited approval process; but it made our advertising decision making work better. After establishing, maybe earning, a trust-based track record, we collapsed decision-making levels. Our agency was more inspired by the trust placed in us to make sure that our work was on target.

That collapsed review/approval process does happen when there is an "owner/operator" of a business, a CEO who has earned personal authority to make advertising decisions. I encountered them in smaller to midsized companies that were still nimble and entrepreneurial. This style needs a boss who listens and staff who is willing to point out if things get off track. The larger the organization, the more risks seem to emerge and need to be addressed.

That streamlined decision making is more often an aberration from the norm. Most companies use their middle management as a filtering system to reduce risks. That is their function. In many ways, it is in opposition to approving good advertising. Advertising, if it is any good, is always risky by nature.

We worked with a government agency to develop an advertising campaign, and we did a considerable, probably excessive amount of pretesting of the advertising selling messages for three campaigns. Only one was going to be used. Why be excessively thorough?

Many times, in organizations, the testing process is less diagnostic and more decision protection. It allows the executives to make decisions based on the research without having to exercise any judgment or responsibility of their own. They would be able to defend the decision by quoting the research to their superiors at the government agency. Being safe is a middle management goal. In fairness, it is also a goal of all government agencies. They need to be able to defend their actions under scrutiny, so they are not in a position to make a daring decision. In many organizations, deniability for mistakes is more important than achievement. As I have said before, success has many parents; failure is an orphan.

When taking ideas that rely on cultural assumptions forward, it is a very good idea to keep in mind the background of the personnel that you are asking to give you approval. As an agency worker, we always kept in mind the WHO who was going to approve the work. While we would like to believe that people make their decisions objectively, we know in all the discussion, from the beginning of this book, that they do not. If you want to get your work approved and produced, you must keep in mind the background, the agenda, the experience, and other characteristics of the people who are going to approve the work. They come with their own biases and inconsistencies, even if they don't know or admit it. Again, reviewing the strategy to set up meetings can help shed some of this baggage, but not all. Even if it is a commonly held belief of your target audience, don't mock Harvard, for example, if the person who has to approve the work went to that school.

Back to the process ladder the work must climb. Once an idea has cleared the hurdles of agency and client approval, depending on the product category, there may be external clearances and approvals required, such as network continuity clearances. Broadcasters don't want to shock or insult their audiences or be liable to claims made on their stations. Their audiences and even their broadcast licenses can be at risk—both of these are dear to the hearts of all broadcasters and get their complete attention.

Tracking this process is like playing the old game of snakes and ladders. You move ahead step by step and then if you hit a roadblock, you must regroup, revise, and start climbing up the chain again through the same steps. It can wear you down or wear the work down into a bland compromise instead of a daring idea. It is important to be steadfast and not cave in.

Through most of this process, decisions are made based on risks and rewards. Usually, the rewards start the process, and they are worn down over time by the risks that people and organizations wish to avoid. There are more opportunities to say "no" than there are to say "yes" as an idea goes through this process. If you think someone has a good idea and "blamo!" it goes on the air, you are badly mistaken. Development work is usually being done months in advance, even for situations where it appears spontaneous. There are just too many elements to put into place to get anything done.

The approval process tends to put a damper on being too provocative. Middle managers who have to approve the ads do not like to take risks with their careers. Their principal function is generally to reduce organizational risk. Being provocative, on the contrary, means taking a risk, so conflict and uneasiness ensues.

From a risk avoidance point of view, the use of a campaign idea can help get a lot of commercials approved more quickly. When a new campaign idea is being presented, options are thought through for various alternative anticipated uses. A campaign is basically a format that can be followed, with variations, to allow a fresh story to be presented to the target that is similar, yet different.

For larger advertisers, these commercials are often produced at one time as a pool, that is two, three, or four commercials can be produced at once. That is why one consideration for evaluating an idea is whether it can be extended, or pooled-out.

There are economic, psychological, and logistical benefits in doing this, which we will discuss in the next chapter. It is also easier to gain management approval for any one member of a campaign pool, that is a group of similar commercials, than any "one off," stand-alone commercial. There is less risk with each member of a commercial pool in a campaign because it is not that different than the one that was already approved. The first is the prototype, after that you are in production. The commercials based on existing campaign ideas are called pool-outs.

The idea of brand trust is enhanced by having a consistent voice and format. The consumer quickly recognizes the format and brand. From an operational basis, the pool of commercials can be approved in one meeting and subsequent pool-outs have less risk because the format being followed has already been endorsed by senior management.

Like most things, when you are making more than one at a time, there are some economic benefits as well, especially if the shoot is well planned. It will depend on how different the commercials in the pool are. The greater the differences, the less the savings.

The obvious question, if you have a pool of two or three commercials, is how do you run them, or in agency jargon: what is the pool rotation policy? We have produced pools of commercials that feature different flavors, different products, different uses, or the same product and use. How you rotate them and how you manage them should be decided.

We have had commercial pools where we all felt that one pool member was much stronger once we saw the finished production. In those cases, we scheduled that commercial for heavier rotation, perhaps two-thirds for one of two members and one-third for the other. There is no set rule to run pool members equally.

There are benefits to having more than one commercial to run. Each commercial wears out slower when there are others in the pool. Think of it like rotating tires.

With long-running campaigns that required quite a few commercials, we did analyses to help understand the wear out of commercials. We looked at the frequency of viewing commercials by the heaviest viewing quartile. That is, we could determine the reach and frequency of any particular commercial in our pool, then look at the frequency that the commercial was seen by the highest viewing quartile (the one quarter of the audience who saw the most exposures). We felt that the risk of wear out would most likely occur in this group. We set a target average frequency of 12 exposures in this heavy-viewing group. Since this group is not a unit but a distribution, we realized that some in it may see the commercial more than 20 times and others less. We set these targets as guidelines using our judgment based on the style of the commercials. Different types of commercials may be more acceptable and effective with more exposures. Think about old television shows or movies. Some you could watch over and over and still enjoy, others—once is maybe enough.

When we reviewed the use of humor, we mentioned that gags or jokes don't wear as well as warm humor. Commercials that have a depth of meaning, multiple levels of interpretation, can last longer and retain their effectiveness. They are able to keep the fast brain fascinated.

Sponsorship opportunities can almost require a pool of commercials. For example, if you are sponsoring a local sporting event and the media package you are required to buy allots you five announcements in the game. Running the same commercial over and over five times yields a diminishing benefit after three times. By the fifth time, the same commercial is almost dysfunctional and causing viewer irritation. Running two or more similar commercials would significantly reduce this risk, even if one is just a reedit of another.

Why would marketers only produce one commercial, then? Cost.

The cost of producing a commercial or an ad is overhead. It is a cost you must make before you can start an advertising program. The more money you can put into media as part of your advertising program, the more pressure you can put on potential buyers to get out and buy your product or service. We do think about media weight as social pressure. Remember when your mother said, "How many times have I told you…"? She wasn't asking for a frequency number from you as the heavy listening quartile. She was reminding you that her repetition is social pressure for you to do something.

One of the conundrums of advertising is the amount of leverage a creative idea has versus the additional pressure that more media spending can provide.

The media pressure seems usually to be quite linear. That is, the more money you put into media the more people are reached with additional frequency. The better the advertising is targeted, as well, the more results you should get. It creates psychological pressure.

Creative ideas are harder to quantify, but they can have a lot more leverage if they are right. They do need repetition to be effective, so enough money has to go to media to make sure that people see the advertising. However, a bland message repeated can only rely on the power of the media pressure to create attitude change.

A breakthrough creative idea can gather social momentum itself and create a lot more attitude change through inspiring customer action. It needs far less media weight to achieve its goals. The problem is usually recognizing when an idea has that social power. There is a real-life story of experienced marketers not being able to recognize that, in Chapter 12. It is not always easy for anyone before the advertising goes on air, but it is always obvious long afterward to many people who claim they knew it all along. It is like picking the Super Bowl champion after the game.

At the beginning of the dot com madness, some companies famously decided to spend their entire budget airing one commercial on a high viewing even like the Super Bowl to stimulate people into talking about their company. Their dream was for their commercial to "go viral."

This is the same kind of dream that every bar band has of becoming the Beatles with even lower odds. This is a highly risky strategy if you are putting a lot of millions just behind the purchase of the time. You are betting your mortgage on the dice coming up 11. The odds of that are 1 in 18 or 5.5 percent. The odds of a commercial going viral are far less. The odds are far greater that the commercial will be forgotten in a week.

The Super Bowl commercials have become a watchable program of their own. It is an expensive bet. Most evaluate the commercials that run only on their entertainment value. Which ones were funny? Which ones had precious moments? Which ones had unexpected turns or surprises? What famous actors were in them? It has diverted the creative development away from the goal of selling the product. The high levels of attention and awareness that is gained have value for getting brands to the top of consumers' minds. Awareness has value. Top of mind awareness has even greater value. But does the cost equal the cost of a Super Bowl ad placement?

The one positive thing for betting heavily on a high attention event is that the fast brain is already fully engaged and paying attention, so you don't have to work too hard to break through. However, there are many better ways of doing that. I encourage risk in advertising, but controlled risk that has thorough thinking behind it, not dice tosses.

The cost of producing a professional national commercial is in the same neighborhood as one prime time national television announcement, or about $100,000.

They are not equivalent, because producing a commercial depends greatly on the idea behind it and the production requirements. It is where the average belies the distribution, as averages often do. Locally produced commercials at the local TV station might only be in thousands of dollars; big-time productions with celebrities on location can go way over that to a million dollars or more.

When we look at media markets much smaller than the huge U.S. national footprint, such as in Europe, Canada, Australia, or others, the cost of producing the advertising starts to be multiples of the cost of airing the commercial.

When media audiences are smaller, based on the cost per thousand in the audience, the announcements cost less to air. That means in smaller markets, commercials run at much higher levels of frequency. Advertisers must amortize their production cost for a longer period. Audiences have adjusted to that fact. The same occurs in local markets in the United States where cost per announcements are low and as a result, as a portion of the advertising budget, production costs are a higher portion. The economies of the audience scale are lost in the smaller media markets.

This is an advantage for franchises or chains that can produce advertising for many stores at once and provide them with creative support. Having worked with a few chains, I can say that not all franchisees feel positively about the creative support that is provided to them by head offices. But when they consider the cost and quality of local production, the advantage of some compromise in using the national creative is very apparent.

Local franchisees also use commercial donuts to provide local deals. These are not sugary baked goods, but commercials with holes or gaps in them for the local franchisees to insert information about local offers or events. This is a win–win situation where the franchisor can control the brand message and the franchisee can tailor immediate sales or location information.

Signing on to a franchise chain means yielding most of the communications to the franchisor. It provides the local franchisee considerably more brand power that they would otherwise have and reduces their production costs for advertising materials.

In these cases, the approval process has been centralized and franchisees often do not have a choice of opting into a program or not. Larger franchisor organizations have libraries of created material that can be drawn on by franchisees or franchisee associations comprised of in-store material, outdoor posters, and print ads that are already produced. This gives chains advantages over local competitors who cannot amortize their production cost over hundreds or thousands of stores.

Franchisee associations are another way of reducing the cost of creating programs and materials. A group of franchisees in a geographic area, usually defined by media coverage, band together in a co-op to support promotions and events. I have worked with a wide range of these, from Toyota dealers each who have businesses with $100 million in sales to Subway franchisees with less than a million. Our agency has even helped the franchisors explain the collective benefits of working together and helped organize some of these advertising trusts.

Even though the scale is different based on the size of the businesses, the benefits of working with fellow franchisees saves money and helps with decision making. It also unifies the public voice.

Franchisors generally encourage these associations. The franchisors are using the franchisees' money to promote the franchisor's brand. This should translate into more sales, increasing the value of the franchise for the franchisee and improving the franchisor's ability to sell franchises. Advertising can build sales and build wealth.

Key Elements for Chapter 8: Advertising Approval Process Challenges

- The process of approval can erode selling ideas.
- There are many people in the approval process who can say "no" and many steps to take from initiating an idea to final approval.
- Respond to significant challenges but resist change for change's sake. Kill the Kilroy.
- Approval through organizations requires the same kind of preparation as preparing advertising: know what your target is thinking, know who they are, know what their goals are, and tell them what the advertising can do for them.
- Don't use research as an alternative to making decisions.
- Campaigns make it easier for approval of any individual piece of advertising.

CHAPTER 9

Production Adversity

Being Prepared for the Unexpected
Requires Attention to Detail

Now that you have your advertising created on paper, you have to produce it in a form that allows you to disseminate it easily to your large target audience. Translating from paper to digital, video, audio, or print can sometimes be easy and seamless. At least, we always hope for that.

Remember the line that "in theory there is no difference between theory and practice, but in practice there is." Every initial piece of advertising is a prototype. It means adversity can and does appear in the road. Be prepared. There are challenges in breaking a new ground.

Producing advertising requires coordinating the actions of a lot of people and bringing a lot of divergent skills into the mix. When you are shooting commercials, you deal with a group of people who have often never worked together before; you may have a new director, new director of photography (DP), new actors, new writer and art director, new producer, new crew, and probably at a new location where none of them have shot before. This kind of work, everyday, requires an openness to problem-solving and improvisation.

I mentioned producing pools of commercials in one production job. This is where some production efficiency comes in. It is also helpful when your acting cast has limited availability. I mentioned shooting with rock stars who always seem to be on tour somewhere promoting their music, or in a studio creating more product to sell. This was the story with Def Leppard who we only had for one day. Each of the rock acts had very limited availability. We designed our production to shoot different sections of the commercials. That only required the stars for short durations. Scenes were shot in different places at different times.

The scenes were later assembled to give the impression that the stars were in those places. We had to plan our production around this.

When shooting with some celebrities, their endorsement contract specifies how many days you might have them available, say in any given year. With Bill Cosby, for example, we ganged three commercials to shoot in two days, allowing us an extra commercial over the two shoot days. We only had six shoot days during the year. There was also efficiency in crew time since we used the same studio for all three commercials.

Using the same crew in a pool means everyone knows their role and can operate much more efficiently as the shoot goes on. Since commercials are one-of-a-kind, there is not much economy of scale. Shooting a pool of commercials, or recording a pool of radio commercials, affords some savings.

All these people who have been brought together for your shoot must immediately work like a well-coordinated team to get the commercial produced. Sometimes only for one day. A lot of crews get attached to a director or DP, which makes working together easier for them. Time is the essence, since some of them may be working somewhere else the next day. It is quite amazing that we actually end up with a finished product with so many cooks in the kitchen.

How is it that these people are all new to each other? Depending on the script for the commercial, the production is bid out, often to three companies who are considered capable of getting the result that the creative team is looking for. Their production bids are reviewed, and a winning bidder is selected. The bids are a combination of costs and creative vision, so the lowest bidder is not always selected.

Shooting commercials takes planning. Formal structured preproduction meetings should come before shooting. These meetings include: client, agency staff, writer, art director, agency producer, director, and sometimes the DP.

At preproduction meetings, every detail that can be anticipated should be reviewed beginning with the script. I also like to start by rereading the strategy aloud just to keep the fast brain framework live. After reviewing the script, the director usually walks everyone through his/her vision of the commercial, the shots, the actors' roles, and the timing of shots. The director may also present a "shooting script," which has the timings marked out.

The actors, their wardrobe, and any props are also reviewed. We prefer to use color-corrected packaging, which is easier for the camera to see for television. We remove all the "mouse print" on the packaging: the ingredients, weights, best by dates, everything but the brand name, and any graphics needed to confirm the look of the package. In normal video-viewing conditions, the mouse print details will not be legible anyway and they can distract from the brand and label. The color-corrected package is usually present at the preproduction meeting for everyone's approval.

Production timing is also reviewed—the shoot date and locations, the rough-cut delivery date, the approval dates, and where and when the client will see the rough cut. If there is an original music track, it is included in the discussion. If possible, it is best to have the original music track available before editing begins so that the cuts can be coordinated with the music rhythm. Stock music can be added later. Stock music is prerecorded selections that can be bought for a fraction of the cost of custom-composed and recorded tracks. There is so much stock written to 30 seconds for commercial use, one or more can often be found, or edited, to match and enhance the video action.

The kind of attention to detail at a preproduction meeting may seem over the top, but it pays off by eliminating questions that may disrupt the shooting day. An ounce of preparation can mean the difference between getting the shots you want or not. It is best to discuss any questions or address any issues before the "golden time" of the shoot day. Overtime can be extremely expensive if you must go beyond the normally booked day.

One secret to success among people who have only just met is a chain of command that should be followed to avoid conflict and confusion. The director is in charge of the production and the crew. Most directors are open to questions and suggestions, but all these comments and questions should be filtered through the agency producer, or if there is no agency producer, then the creative team.

It is a collaborative process, so there are lots of conversations about shots happening all the time, but there is only one channel through which these should be brought forward. Many times, we have had clients worried about a shot or a take and wanting to say something. I usually counsel patience. Let the creative team figure out the issue, the blocking, the lighting, the camera angle, before interrupting their process. When you are doing something for the first time, rarely do you get it right on the first attempt. Every commercial is doing something for the first time. Interruptions slow the process down and can cost a lot. As I mentioned before, don't buy a dog, and bark yourself.

Despite all the careful planning, things can go seriously awry.

When we had Def Leppard for one day in April in Montreal on a stop of their North American tour, we planned a half-day shoot outdoors for our commercial. We did not expect five inches of fresh snow on that single day they were available. We did a quick script rewrite to be able to shoot the group in a rapidly arranged studio staged to match the rest of the commercial which would be shot outdoors.

My good friend, creative director Mike Hart, was shooting a Nestle coffee commercial in Jamaica. The commercial focused on a yacht and the beautiful Jamaican countryside, which was the backdrop to talk about the coffee's origins. Mike and his team got to their remote area in Jamaica with the crew, the actors, and the client when the Jamaican government increased the price of gasoline. There was a national strike in protest to the crippling increase; highways and roads were blocked. No one was allowed into the area where the Nestle shoot was to take place. No yacht was going to be arriving to star in the commercial shoot.

The group was ready to abandon the shoot, write it off, and just try to get back safely to North America since the opportunity seemed to be lost. They were fortunate enough to have the genius of Hart with them; he was fortunate enough to have the client there. He had the approved creative strategy; the client, the talent, and the crew. So, he calmly sat down and wrote a new commercial without the yacht in it. With the client there to approve the new script, they went on. The shoot was then based on the new script and the new commercial was produced. Anticipating events like this just isn't possible.

A similar problem happened to me when a General Foods (GF) commercial was to be shot at a remote jungle location. For personal reasons, I couldn't be there, although we did do a thorough preproduction meeting, so I felt things were under control. When I saw the footage, there were sections of the approved script that had not been shot.

The client was rightly very upset. We took the footage we had and put together a new commercial using that footage. It was quite different from the one approved. It made sense because it was true to the approved strategy and delivered on the brand's promise. It was approved to go on air. A surprise, but an effective commercial.

One Mr. Clean commercial, back in the age of film, the raw film was loaded incorrectly in the developer and ended up with sprocket holes in it. That necessitated a new shoot paid for by completion insurance. Having insurance for your shoot is always a good idea.

There was difficulty in getting the actors and crew back together for a new shoot date. When we finally found a date that worked, the actress who had been our lead character originally had decided to get her upper lip bleached because she thought it showed some mustache hair. She showed up with an extremely red, swollen upper lip that even make-up couldn't solve.

Luckily, our alternate casting choice was available and could get to the studio within a of couple hours while we shot product demonstrations. The substitute did a superior job.

And on the subject of upper lips, for a Wendy's promotion commercial, we hired a famous hockey player, Eddie Shack, who was very well known for his giant handlebar mustache. He was to do a close-up biting into a Wendy's sandwich, very close-up. The commercial used vignettes and some bouncy music to show a range of famous people enjoying the sandwich.

Shack was so excited to be in a commercial, he wanted to look his best. To do so, he shaved off his mustache. Now he was not recognizable; he was just a guy with a big nose. Our makeup person built a new mustache for his upper lip. She did an amazing job in little time. We were fine to go. As a joke, we did a final shot where he ripped off the fake mustache to bite the sandwich, as if nothing could get in his way in enjoying the food.

The shot was hilarious; our client loved it. We used it as the final cut of the commercial that went on air. It was unexpected. I then got calls from industry media asking if he was the real Eddie Shack, or just a look alike. No problem. People had noticed the provocative twist from the expected and later the commercial won an award. Making lemonade when you are handed lemons.

We never expect these kinds of potential disasters to happen. In fact, we dread it when they do. I have mentioned a few; there were many more. When they do happen, the important thing to remember is to remain calm and look for a solution that lets you move forward. Sitting in misery or feeling sorry for your bad luck is not a way out. Anyone working in the commercial production business has a lot of these stories. Who expects five inches of snow in April? Fine! What is our backup plan? How do we work around it?

I mentioned that testimonials can be tricky to produce, nevertheless, a good one can be very powerful, because it features a product user's experience in a trustworthy way. It often includes little details that are unique to that user, which help make the story much more believable and much less fabricated, as a result more convincing the target. Details like little Georgie's cherry tree.

We had an excellent radio testimonial for a detergent that our legal advisers said we could not use. However, the story was really interesting, in a regional dialect, and quite idiosyncratic. It was charming and we didn't want to lose it. We had the user give us a release to use her story and her name, but we could not use her voice.

Since we still wanted to use the story, we prepared a transcript of her telling of the story and hired a voice actress to rerecord the story. Studio time was booked and away we went. The actress did a very good job; we recorded the copy five or six times, but she still sounded, to us, like the copy was not in her words, like she was reading a script. We didn't want listeners to think it was not her honest story. Without letting her prepare further, we went into the studio and spoke with her. That wasn't unexpected; it happens all the time. We asked if she was clear about the story, and she was.

Then, unexpectedly, we asked for her copy of the script, took it away from her, and left the studio. Back in the control room, she was asked to tell us the story in the regional style we were looking for. Without having the script in front of her, she told us as if the story had happened to her. It was much more believable with a lot more power.

Taking the script away after half dozen reads allowed her to escape from being an announcer and go into being a character. While we had been forced into this by the unusual situation, I have used the technique many times since then, when I thought a voice actor was sounding too much like an announcer and less like a person speaking to us from their own experience.

Listeners want to overhear the truth being spoken, not a motivated prepared message trying to convince them of something or fool them. It is about credibility.

This technique was one way of overcoming the bias that comes with hearing a motivated message. The motivated message just isn't as believable. Did I tell you I was great? Or did Shirley? Or did you overhear it from someone on an elevator.

One technique that appears obvious in some testimonial commercials is when the customer has been too rehearsed and prepared. They are filmed reading from a telepromoter or an off-camera script. The reading, more often than not, is wooden and unbelievable. Tonality and cadence are key.

As they say, "if you can't fake sincerity, what can you do?" When the message is clearly motivated, it is not credible. Go back to Chapter 4 and read it again.

I hear a lot of people complaining about casting in television commercials. The allegation is based on the assumption that advertisers are forcing more minority performers into commercials.

Advertising is not a political trendsetter. Products are inanimate objects and have no sense of who is buying them. Marketers also generally don't care who is buying as long as there is a sale.

Our direction in casting for a commercial is to make sure it reflects the market that the product is looking for. Who is buying? We want viewers to see the commercial as showing someone that could be them getting a benefit from the product. We want the audience to empathize and model their behavior accordingly. We want to sell the product. If advertising gets sidetracked by trying to make a political statement, it is not achieving its goal and doing its economic or social work.

I particularly have liked to cast people who were ethnically ambiguous. This allows many more people in the audience to empathize with the person in the ad or commercial. The actors can represent whoever in the audience thinks they look like, hopefully them. That's inclusion.

Marketers generally want sales, not political action. If you think otherwise, you have never been a marketer responsible for sales results, with your year-end bonus depending on the results.

The exception to this is the ego-driven owner as described in the Five Peaces, Part II in the Appendix. Their behavior subverts advertising from its real purpose.

Diversity is great if it doesn't look forced or contrived; then it is a motivated message from an advertiser. It works well if it reflects a changing society. Showing a variety of types of people might open markets for your product. Look at where your sales are coming from and get an idea of ethnic correlations to purchasers. If the correlations are there, reflect those purchasers or users in your ads, or even consider parallel campaigns in ethnic media.

One way to handle diversity of your customer base is to vary the ethnic mix and product usage is through "pool-outs" as part of a campaign. When an ad is created, it is usually put through a pool-out test. Is the commercial a stand-alone idea or can it be iterated into more commercials keeping the same idea and look and feel but being refreshed in some ways? I have mentioned a few long-running campaigns; they were all cookie cutters of an original idea, with variations. These allow the advertiser to evolve their message while remaining familiar.

That consistency and familiarity make the message nonthreatening to the fast brain.

Campaigns

When we begin a conversation, you expect me to be the same person from start to finish. The same is true for brands. Advertising should be seen as a long series of conversations by the brand with the customer.

A new commercial requires a learning curve, starting with recognition and orientation. Who is telling me this? What is this about? It takes a moment, once we have your attention, for your fast brain to understand and then digest the message. Learning theory says that the more often the message is repeated, the more the viewer understands, comprehends the idea, and becomes competent in it.

I have spent a lot of time doing advertising to children. They see repetition differently than adults do. Kids are watching people and actions, learning to master ideas and skills. They are personally rewarded by both the learning of an idea and the satisfaction of mastering the information.

That is why children enjoy seeing movies again and again. The satisfaction for them comes from knowing what is going to happen, to demonstrate, if only to themselves, that they have learned the lesson. They have learned and mastered what the characters are going to do next and often what the dialogue is going to be. That mastery is very satisfying to kids.

In some campaigns, we worked at creating parallel story lines and humor on multiple levels of sophistication, so different age groups could see and master different plots. Kids under six like the slapstick and physical humor. Older kids, with more engaged language skills in their fast brain, can understand puns and word jokes. Kids who are even older understand the socially based humor that is totally lost on the little kids. By designing the commercials to have at least these levels of meaning, we could reach age ranges with the same commercials.

I mentioned the power that Bill Cosby had with parents and kids. The rules for television advertising are that you cannot use well-known celebrities to advertise to children. The understanding is that the authority that celebrities have with kids can put undue pressure on those kids. Political pressure led to the networks restricting the use of celebrities in advertising to kids.

We couldn't use astronauts to pitch Tang to kids. We developed a campaign using moon creatures who tried to convince NASA to send more astronauts to the moon because more astronauts would bring them more Tang.

For JOP we did a lot of exploring of campaigns to reach kids directly, but we didn't have a large budget, so we hoped that kids would see Cosby's commercials in adult shows. We scheduled more of our weight on television earlier in the evening when kids would be more likely to be watching but not be a majority of the audience, which would classify the time slots as Kids television. Generally, only the weekend mornings gained that classification and restrictions.

Making sure you are speaking the language of your prospects is important. The more the advertising speaks to them on the same level as they are and in the same kind of language they use, the more familiar and trustworthy the advertising will be. The more understandable it will be and the more clarity it will have. Adults are just grown-up kids— some are at the slapstick level; some understand the word play; some see the social meaning and the deeper ideas. Your audience's speech and look will also vary by class, ethnicity, and region; make sure that commercial casting reflects who you want them to be identifying as.

The goal in producing the on-paper message is to take it to a richer level. The same way the designing of the message should elevate the creative strategy to be more understandable and motivating. Advertisers should want the fast brain to embrace the produced message and identify with the solution that is proposed in it; not be distracted by some production element such as looks, speech pattern, or fashion incongruities. It has to look real.

Key Elements for Chapter 9: Production Adversity

- Make sure all members of the team have reviewed and agreed to production choices.
- Plan a thorough preproduction meeting and review all elements before production.

- Consider shooting pools of commercials to save on costs and time.
- Productions are done by teams of mostly strangers who haven't worked together before. It gets done by people sticking to their roles.
- Follow the chain of command at a production. The director is in charge.
- Be prepared for unanticipated eventualities. They can come from anywhere. Always have a back-up plan and always build in extra time to handle delays and hiccups.
- Make slice-of-life production appear as real to life as possible to make it easier for the target audience to believe. If it is not believed, it won't be persuasive.
- Actors can make commercials believable or ineffective advertiser-motivated messages. There is a big difference in the impact on the audiences.
- Casting of voices or actors should reflect the typical users of the product to make empathy easier for the audience that the advertising is addressed to.
- Campaigns should look like a consistent family of messages, not disparate ones.

CHAPTER 10

Assessing the Results

Advertising Is a Long-Term Dialogue
Between the Product and Its Users

Once your advertising is released to public exposure, you will get more feedback. It will come from all quarters, and *like the attributes of your product, not all will be benefits for you*, the user of the advertising. Keep your eye on the original goal that was set for the advertising. That should be the basis for all evaluation of the advertising.

Kahneman points out that people will often avoid a hard question and answer a derivative one that is easier. When the commercial was being shot, someone didn't like the wardrobe, or the way an actor delivered a line, or a legal requirement. Once you are on the air with a commercial, ignore those comments or doubts if they are brought up again. They are irrelevant and in the past; they are easy answers that avoid the real question: is the advertising achieving its goal.

If sales are responding, if that was the goal, the rest of the blather and Monday morning quarterbacking is just useless background crowd noise.

Not all advertising starts with a bang in terms of consumer response. There is a learning curve for the audience that doesn't respond with only little exposure to an idea. It gets steeper with more exposure and repetition. It takes a while for those exposed to new ideas to learn what is being said to them. Generally, a minimum of three exposures is required for a target audience to be able to comprehend and absorb the new advertising idea. That means each member of the audience must see a commercial or ad three times to be influenced. This is a guide; this means *average*. Viewers who are heavier users of media, watch more TV or video, listen to more radio, read more periodicals, will see ads much more often.

This is not the equivalent to airing a commercial three times since only a small percentage of the target audience will see every airing. We measure this as Reach (percentage who see it) and Frequency (how many times on average the audience will see it). Patience is required by the advertiser until the audience has had a chance to see and absorb the advertising selling idea.

Beware: An advertising idea may no longer seem new to the advertiser, because that advertiser has been living with it for many months. Give it time. When an advertiser is putting a new idea forward, it takes a while to make an impact on the audience. This new advertising idea is not the only area of interest in the audience's lives. They will have much less interest to focus on the advertising than the advertiser has had. Remember the steps required: being provocative enough to be noticed, getting the audience to remember it, and making sure it was well branded, clear, credible, and convincing enough to generate some action. Don't expect these steps to be instantaneous. They are usually deliberate.

The data gurus tell us that deep analyses of returns on marketing spending indicate that advertising can initially be a cost with little returns, but over time the cumulative building of awareness and preference pay back handsomely.[1] Many advertisers would confirm that, as would our case study story in Chapter 12. All the pointers say: if you have done your homework well, stay the course and you will build brand wealth. It takes time for the awareness and preferences to seep into the slow consumer brain.

However, the patience of the people working on advertising is often put to test. When the advertisers become habituated to the campaign, it starts to become boring, just background noise. They perceive its excitement and effectiveness to have diminished. In my experience, patience runs out quicker at the agencies because their role, purpose, and priority is to come up with new ideas. It is part of the agency identity. If they are not pitching new ideas, they worry that they will lose the client. Their logical brain understands that it is better to have a client getting good sales results, but when the fast brain itches, it is hard not to scratch.

Patience next runs low for the advertiser. Particularly, if there has been a change in personnel at a senior level in managing the advertising or marketing programs. Advertisers tend to be driven by results and it is hard for driven individuals to put their drive into neutral and wait. If sales haven't responded strongly enough, the individual's patience kicks into gear.

All managers want to put their stamp on what the public sees of their work. Few resumés brag that "I kept the campaign I inherited running and saw sales continue to grow." Why? Because we all think that taking leadership means making changes. Everyone seems doomed to making sure they left their mark on their assignments. Like Kilroy was here.

I have seen more campaigns changed and agencies changed, often for no good reason, when new client staff came on board. We were working with another oil company (not Texaco) when a new vice president of marketing was appointed. Our agency had recently been evaluated and given their highest ratings for our work to that point. Nevertheless, within six months an agency review was called where we would pitch against other agencies for retention of the account.

When I asked our regular contact at the company if our agency should even compete, he was shocked. He replied that we had just been evaluated very highly and were odds on favorites to retain the business. I replied that we were not evaluated highly enough to avoid an agency review.

I was inclined not to compete, not to waste our team's efforts and morale on a losing proposition. Our team wouldn't hear of it. It was an important account for us, and we all wanted to keep it. We pitched very well ... and lost—"you were a close second" was what our contact told me. In competitions where there is only one winner, being second is equivalent to being 43rd. It is usually binary, in or out.

Advertisers, be patient. A watched pot is slow to boil. It is more efficient to work with your campaigns, to evolve them if they are not performing up to expectations. Talk to customers to see if you can find weaknesses to address. Change is change; there is no guarantee it is for the better even though that is always our hope.

I mentioned the Subway breakfast launch we did. Let me add a little anecdote about it to understand comments we get on our advertising. Before I do, let me remind you that the commercial was entirely successful in launching the new day part for Subway and used in various countries around the world.

Shortly after the commercial went on the air, I was shopping with my young son for office supplies at a big box store. I talk to everyone I meet, much to my son's disapproval. When we got to the cashier, we chatted. The cashier asked me what I did, and I told her I made commercials.

"So, what have you done that I might have seen?" she asked, with a somewhat inquiring yet dismissive demeanor.

"We just aired a commercial for Subway," I said, "introducing their breakfast."

"Oh yeah?" she said, rapidly adding, "Is that the commercial where the girl wakes up late and has problems with her contact lens. And then she has to dodge some dogs while she's walking down the street? And then she goes into a Subway for breakfast and some guy gives her the eye and smiles at her? Well, I have been into Subway, and I have tried their breakfast, and it was really good," she said, finally drawing a breath.

"Terrific!" I replied.

"…but your commercial sucks!" she added.

"Huh?" I said, taking in a surprised breath myself, "What do you mean?"

"That girl! Why did you choose that girl? She has a big nose!"

As we walked out, my young son looked up at me and said, "She didn't like your commercial."

Meanwhile, I was thinking: she had remembered the commercial; she had incredible recall of many of the details of the commercial; she had even been motivated enough to go to a Subway for breakfast; she bought the product; she liked the product! Wow! The commercial was a total success converting this potential Subway customer.

For me this was a grand slam home run. The commercial had been provocative, memorable, well branded, clear, credible, and convincing enough to gain trial. It successfully launched Subway's breakfast business with the cashier.

And I did not think the actress we used had a big nose. But if casting an actress with a big nose is what it takes for the reception I heard from the cashier, I am all for it.

I get these kinds of "expert" comments all the time from people who have seen the tip of the iceberg and have no real understanding for what goes into putting the advertising together. I once got into an argument with a person at a party who really liked one of our television commercials. It was for Prestone Antifreeze. He thought it was a great commercial, he liked the visualizing of the benefit, the acting, and was complementing me. So why were we arguing then?

The argument started when I told him we hadn't used TV for Prestone for years, that it had been a radio commercial he was describing to me. He again described in great detail what he was sure he had "seen." But he hadn't. He refused to believe me and preferred his version of reality over the facts. (Sounds familiar?) False memories can be as realistic and vivid as real ones.

I shrugged and thought what a great radio commercial it was since it created an entire video in the listener's imagination—we call it theater of the mind. It got through his fast brain and created an entire scenario in his slower logical brain where deeper memories can be stored. A scenario he could recall and describe, even if it didn't happen. A fabricated memory can be as good or better than a real one. It convinced him about the product.

Everyone has an opinion of the commercials we make. Most use their fast brains to evaluate the commercials on superficial elements. As Kahneman said, it is easier to answer an easy question that wasn't asked than to answer a hard question that was.

If your commercial gets check marks for the criteria we have gone through, stick with it. Any coach will tell you that it is blocking and tackling that wins the game, not the outlier "Hail Mary pass." If you hit your marks, the statistics say you will eventually win more than you will lose. The Casinos know this. That's why they lose or stay even in the short run, but over the longer run they always win.

Don't be lured away by the shiny objects and doubt your plan.

Advertisers should always play for the long run, if they can, although sometimes politics get in the way. Work to building a long-term dialogue with your prospects and customers for your brand through advertising. Be consistent in how the brand is presented; make it familiar and trustworthy to the public. That is how to build a customer base.

The passing grades or better don't come from one exam, but from doing the right kind of dedicated work throughout the course of the advertising campaigns. Each ad presented to the public is part of that continuing conversation and if advertisers are consistently getting check marks on the elements that sell the product, making the advertising message clear and empathetic, advertisers will get results.

Key Elements for Chapter 10: Assessing the Results

- Once the advertising is produced, put doubts about development and production behind you.
- Don't listen to random comments from so-called experts.
- Assess the results against the stated goals in the creative strategy.
- Advertising builds as it disseminates to the public. Long-term returns are more important than any short-term reactions.
- Advertising campaigns wear out inside marketing departments and agencies quicker and more often than with the target audiences.
- Don't change your advertising just because there was a personnel change.
- Marketers and agencies should sometimes park their egos and put the business ahead of making their own mark.
- Monitor advertising performance against some qualitative measure.
- Stay the course.

CHAPTER 11

Conclusions

Advertising takes disciplined thinking. You won't be successful without imposing that discipline on the process. There is more to the iceberg than the shiny part you see.

Clients have come to us and asked for "something that can go viral." Why? Because they think there is some free ride to a piece of communication that gets passed around independently by other people at no cost to them. We all have hopes and dreams.

Every kid has imagined themselves at bat in the bottom of the ninth inning at an imaginary World Series deciding game. As of this writing, there has been more than a century of World Series. There have only been two walk-off home runs in all that time: Bill Mazeroski in 1960 and Joe Carter in 1993. That is less than 2 percent of all World Series endings.

For those home runs to occur, many other independent events had to happen to set the stage for the dramatic ending. These events were mainly out of the control of the batters. When an advertiser is hoping for a piece of advertising to go viral, it is the same kind of dreamy hope the kid has at their imaginary at bat. Nice to dream about, but not a reasonable goal to aim for or result to expect. Few of us can build success from a 2 percent possibility. Nevertheless, we dream, even if it is unrealistic. Slow brain, help us manage our expectations!

I have worked on a couple of campaigns that went out of paid advertising and into the popular culture. It was great! Advertising is ephemeral; it does not endure long in the public consciousness. Public attention is fickle and fleeting. It goes to the fast brain and that is not a long-term depository of memories. Our home runs were soon forgotten.

Brands, on the other hand, can be built and sustained over a long period of time. Brand names, identities, and promises can be a form of wealth built by advertising over time. Hitting lots of singles, getting on base, advancing those players along—this is a better way to score than hoping for the drama of that 2 percent solution.

For advertising, the difficult part is understanding what the product's real benefit is to prospective customers. That requires a hard look at the product or service that is being provided to see where the product's leverage is with potential buyers. It can be difficult to see the product from the buyer's perspective and understand what the most appealing and motivating feature is. Not just seeing the product from their perspective, but empathizing with them in how they use it, how they talk about it, how it fits into the buyer's life, understanding their WIIFM.

Writing out a clear creative strategy is the kind of discipline needed to keep the goal for advertising in focus. The strategy is the blueprint against which all advertising is built. Always work toward this goal. The strategy is best developed in partnership with the creative team chosen to write your advertising. The place to start to get to a persuasive idea that works, is to start with what the prospective target already believes in their fast, operating brain. Direct messages to this part of audience consciousness.

Confrontations don't persuade because there can only be one winner. The fast brain is quick to defend beliefs. Persuasion changes minds by evolving them.

Developing advertising can easily run off when encountering tangential ideas. Stick to the strategy that has been written. The usual problem with creating advertising isn't creating executional ideas, but getting the right kinds of ideas. These ideas fall in a sweet spot, defined by the strategy, with a message that is provocative, memorable, well branded, clear, credible, and convincing enough to gain traction with the fast brains of the audience. The advertiser can't fight the audience for their opinion; the advertiser must persuade them to consider the selling ideas.

To be credible, the message must show some degree of expertise, be trustworthy, and reduce suspicion that the message is only there for someone else's benefit, the advertiser.

Using language or situations that are contrived and obviously staged, leaves a message that will also be seen as contrived and manipulating.

Here's a fragment from a current commercial: "With my moderate to severe symptoms..." This is nothing anyone would ever say, outside of a commercial; a person either has moderate or severe symptoms. There is one person; there is one condition. So which is it? Lines that are forced or don't seem natural undermine the credibility of the message. Overcoming opposition requires persuasion.

Elevated language, obvious legal caveats like adding the word "brand," anything that seems like unnatural speech sends alarm signals to the audience's brain to either dismiss the message or argue against it. Credibility is assigned by the audience when conditions are right. The advertiser can have considerable control on those conditions. Good acting and voice qualities in commercials allow the audience to believe that the information is more honest and real. The slick announcer is rarely seen as being sincere or honest.

Advertisers need to be able to see and hear their messages the way their audience sees and hears them, not the way advertisers wish they were seen and heard. Empathy is a tough skill to learn. Talking to customers and listening to how they speak is a great way to improve the ad selling power.

When reviewing options for advertising, the most persuasive messages are those that show the product being effective. Inclusion in commercials of what we have called "strategy visuals," which integrate the branded product in a demonstration, improve the advertising's effectiveness. These can become semiotics that instantly telegraph the brand and the solution without any words. They are the grail for advertisers. A clear strategy visual means the audience immediately understands the reason to buy or agree with the selling idea.

Showing people who look like the audience using the product to solve problems makes learning the end benefits or end-to-end benefits easier for the audience to integrate into their lives. Seeing is easier to believe and understand than being told something.

We reviewed a few of the executional options that are often used to package the strategy into a message that is understandable and compelling to the target audience. We also reviewed some of the executional techniques that can be employed to help make messages more provocative, memorable, and easy to understand. There are advantages and disadvantages to all of them.

Advertisers should build on familiar situations and language. The fast brain doesn't want to have to call on the energy needed by the slow brain to figure out a message. The fast brain will just ignore or reject the message.

Address the target's fast brain with clear simple ideas that provoke attention. Advertising may have taken months to develop, but the audience only has a few seconds to assess and decide whether to pay attention or not. If you can come up with a strategy visual that expresses your product and its benefit, use it! Keep using it, dressing it in different clothes by placing it in different situations.

We reviewed the weaknesses of the straightforward voice-over talking to camera. It can be more persuasive as a voice-over while seeing the product in situations solving problems.

Humor can be an effective tool, but it is more effective for advertising when used to create a smile than as a laugh. Jokes are less funny each time we hear them, and advertising must be repetitive. The warmth of the right kind of humor can invite an audience to pay attention and feel familiar with the message, thereby opening the door to attention, retention, and possible action.

If a strategy works in one culture or language, it will likely work in another based on my work in advertising in four languages and multiple cultures. We are all pretty much looking for the same things in life. The languages and some cultural behaviors change in the message execution, but the benefits of products do not. They all answer real needs or fail in the market.

Don't let the corporate approval process erode your strategy or the execution of it in a message. Remember that the decision makers approving ads are also a target audience. Know what their attitudes and beliefs are before pitching them ideas. Make sure to align approval of the advertising with the goals those decision makers have for themselves and their business responsibilities.

The same strategic paradigm can be used talking to decision makers inside the business as you use to talk to potential consumers. The strategy may be different, but the steps are the same: what is the current belief of the manager, what is the goal the brand is trying to achieve, what promise will the advertising deliver on, and why it will work.

Absorb this paradigm to make communication effective. It will work in most situations.

The goal of this book is to guide the reader into creating the right elements to sell their idea, their product, or their service. Hopefully, this results in clear and persuasive messages. Make sure the homework is done to understand the context for that message. One caveat, great advertising is the fastest way to kill a bad product, service, or idea. It will also accelerate acceptance of a good one. The faster more people know the product's benefit, the faster that knowledge will be put into action.

Keep your eye on the goal and don't get sidetracked with secondary goals. Be patient; the world isn't waiting for your message to arrive. Make sure the message is engaging. Keep it simple. Repeat. Keep it simple.

Don't be afraid to seek professional help. You are not Duane. Understanding the required parameters of the message allows you to delegate its creation to those with higher level technical skills. Managing them means making sure they clearly understand the persuasive message you need.

Don't let your work get siloed. Stay open to improvisations as long as they are consistent with your strategy and help deliver it. Advertising is more like jazz than classical scores. Advertisers who work in silos and not holistically might miss this point.

Advertising is not data driven; it is insight driven. Insights can come out of data but so can mediocre ideas. It is about communicating and inspiring your prospects, not pummeling them into submission.

When my friend Duane, the engineer with the PhD who was in the astronaut program, ran for our high school student council, he was smart enough to seek advice on how to do it right. Of course, we won. Now, without help from Duane, go check out this book's Appendix.

For a Recap of Chapter 11: Conclusions

- Advertising goes to your audience's fast brain. That part of the brain provides an immediate assessment and reacts best to the sensory input.
- Look for the end benefit only your product can provide and understand it from its user's point of view.
- Develop a creative strategy starting with the user's accepted belief. Identify the prospective buyers. Promise them an end benefit and explain why your product has it. Put this in writing. Review it often.
- Make sure your offer is going to be believed. Follow the keys to being believable.
- Come up with creative executions with the help of professionals with technical creative skills. Review the options.
- Evaluate whether these are good ideas from the prospects point of view.
- Be careful not to erode the creative idea when taking it through the approval process.
- When producing the message be prepared to hit some adversity, some bumps, and unexpected challenges. Be open to adjusting and pivoting to opportunities, but never swerve from the strategy.
- Always have a backup no matter how confident you feel.

CHAPTER 12

A Real Case Study

We have reviewed a lot of theories with glimpses of sample cases using actual situations that demonstrate areas we have been reviewing.

I would like to share a more detailed case study to show the many challenges and processes that advertising must go through before the audience sees it.

This case is old enough to hopefully keep from offending anyone. However, the situation is still very relevant to the advertising development processes today and not uncommon, except for its exceptional success and tragic end.

The case is notable because the campaign endured successfully for more than 20 years. Not many campaigns last that long, although it is every advertiser's goal to find a campaign idea that can while dramatically increasing sales and build a lasting consumer relationship.

The corporate dynamics and decision making were typical. They demonstrate many of the points that have been reviewed here. It also shows the power of a simple great idea to boost sales of a moribund product with an insight that connected with the audience.

The idea didn't pretest well; the marketers and advertising professionals did not have great faith in it. Patience and the consumer appeal that it built delivered exceptional results.

My advice for anyone who hears "I'll know great advertising when I see it" from a decision maker is to get out of the project as quickly as possible. You are dealing with someone who will waste your time and efforts and has no real ability to understand advertising. Give them a copy of this book to read before you start work. We must articulate our standards to achieve them.

Knowing when advertising is going to be a hit is a random event. I have been involved in campaigns that took off and became pop culture phenomena, but you never know beforehand.

This demonstrates how advertising is developed, tested, and approved through corporate organizations. It should give you an understanding of the pitfalls, ups and downs for creating historically successful advertising.

Jell-O Pudding (JOP) was a tired old GF brand in 1973 when I was first assigned to the account as a junior trainee at Young & Rubicam (Y&R), New York.

One of my first tasks was to do a thorough historic review of JOP advertising and spending going back to the early 1950s, to see if we could learn anything from the brand's history. What had worked and what didn't work? Could we get some insights to guide development of future advertising?

I watched commercials on 16-mm film, even commercials going back to the 1950s on kinescopes (recordings on film taken from TV broadcasts) in black and white. Some were two minutes long, featuring actors and announcers from sponsored shows casually talking about desserts, selling JOP with many sales points (think of product placement with influencers and how they go on about irrelevant attributes). The pacing was originally slow, but evolved and sped up first to one minute, then to 30 seconds over 10 years or so. Actors on sponsored shows ceased pitching and were replaced by commercials not connected to sponsored shows.

The historic analysis did not reveal much. Sales steadily declined from the early 1950s, with an occasional bump from a promotion or the introduction of a new instant form of cooked pudding. There were product improvements advertised regularly without any lasting impact on sales. The strategy that kids loved pudding stayed pretty much the same I thought, although I didn't have old file versions of the written creative strategy.

This review gave me, and then our team when I presented my report, an understanding of the ongoing dialogue that JOP had with its customer base over the decades.

It did not seem to make much difference whether advertising spending increased or declined. The budget, at the time of my report, was relatively small by packaged goods standards, less than $2.5 million per year or about $14 million in today's dollars. The brand was just floating along reminding people that it was there but without generating much excitement. You might conclude that it didn't respond to advertising. The advertising sustained the brand but didn't drive sales.

Despite this, JOP was a prestigious assignment for Y&R with many of the senior management, including the chairman at the time, Ed Ney, having taken a turn at running the business. Some of Y&R's best and brightest had tried.

The brand's advertising strategy and budget was split to provide recipes and usage ideas to homemakers via print ads and use TV to convince consumers that JOP was their kids' favorite dessert. Our TV tag line was "Kids Love Pudding" was very workmanlike.

We knew that mothers were always trying to get their kids to drink more milk, so we showed the product beside a pitcher of milk. It also gave the brand some halo of nutrition and goodness.

The first TV commercial I worked on that year took place at a summer camp. In the commercial, getting JOP made the camp experience positive for the kids because "kids love pudding." The set was tremendous; a complete camp cafeteria had been constructed in a New York City studio. It was an impressive first TV commercial shoot for me to see. So many people running in all directions, so much equipment, lighting, and camera.

A problem that evolved from the shoot later was how much of the budget was spent on the very cinematic set and how little of this set showed up in the final commercial, which was mostly close-ups of kids talking and eating pudding.

The GF client was not impressed with the cost of a set that was hardly seen for a brand with a modest budget. Despite the adversity, and the blemish, the commercial was finished and aired.

The follow-up commercial that was developed featured a kid practicing his trumpet, terribly, off screen. The father and mother were at the kitchen table. The father (played by Charles Durning, later in The Sting, Dog Day Afternoon, Tootsie, etc.) is reading the newspaper and asks the mother if she can do something about the noise. The mother turns and shouts, "Sheldon, I am making you some pudding."

Cutaway to the product story (kids love it; it is made with milk), the brand beauty and package shot with a pitcher of milk.

Back to the family in the kitchen. Sheldon is happily eating his pudding and says, "Hope you've made enough, Tommy's coming over to practice his tuba with me!" At this point, Durning, the father, looks up from his newspaper, rolls his eyes and falls over backward in his chair right onto the floor. Hilarious slapstick moment.

At least we thought it was hilarious.

We presented it for final approval to our senior GF client for the first time, then my boss asked if our client would like to see it again. The client quietly answered he did not. In fact, he said, he did not ever want to see it again and he didn't want anyone else to see it either.

He put JOP TV advertising spending on hold until a replacement campaign could be developed. He obviously did not think the commercial was funny. Given the lack of JOP sales response to advertising over 20 years, it was probably a risk worth taking.

This put the agency into shock. A keystone account had been suspended over a commercial the agency thought was a good one.

A couple of background points may explain the strong difference of opinion here. The mom, played by Marilyn Sokol, had a strong New Yorker accent. When she yelled "Shelllll-don," it sounded like a battle cry from Brooklyn. In those days a New York accent was still considered to sound very "ethnic" and lower class. "New York Ethnic" was a euphemism for Jewish.

While GF looked Midwestern, our client who had to approve the commercial was very much a New Yorker, representing a small minority of non-WASPs in GF's senior management. Approving a commercial that was so "ethnic" might have been seen as a career miscue for him given the corporate environment. The overall corporate view was that their target audiences were, like the company, Midwestern and traditional, not ethnic.

Shortly after this happened, I finished my training period on JOP. I was promoted off the brand and on to other assignments. I worked on Windex, then Tang (Instant Breakfast Drink). Junior executives were rotated on different assignments to get broader experience.

About a year and a half after I had left, JOP was still not advertising on TV. It was just supported by print ads for dessert recipes. Without significant spending on TV, the agency was not making much money on the account, even though the agency had to do all the creative development work and research needed to find a new JOP replacement TV campaign.

A lot of work had been and was being done. Eventually, three JOP TV campaigns emerged and went into testing. One was particularly difficult to test because it featured a well-known celebrity, a comedian named Bill Cosby.

At that time, Cosby was only a stand-up comedian who had considerable success with comedy records (they were a thing then). A few years before the commercial was shot, he had a role as a tennis player, playing undercover spy in a TV show called "I Spy." That made him one of the first African American lead characters on U.S. network TV. Having an African American lead, or colead, was a revolutionary idea in the basically all-white TV environment of the day. He had also just started to voice a newly launched Saturday morning TV cartoon show called "Fat Albert" that was developed from characters in his stand-up comedy material.

Cosby had very high TVQ scores. TVQ was a syndicated industry research tool, which indicated he was both likable and had very good awareness with the public. He had never done any product endorsement TV commercials before, so this was new ground for JOP and for him.

There was a certain amount of nervousness at GF about using an African American as a product spokesman. There were no other brands going this route. Celebrities GF used were more like Robert Young (star of Father Knows Best and Marcus Welby) for Maxwell House; these spokespeople were safe, bland, and well-trusted. Breaking barriers is always uncomfortable and a risky business. No one wants to have it backfire on them.

The Cosby commercial was one of three options under consideration. All were tested using Burke DAR (Day After Recall) scores—our main commercial evaluation tool at the time. The theory was that if no one could remember your commercial the day after it ran, it would not be provocative or memorable enough to sell product.

The DAR methodology was to run a commercial at the exact same time on all three affiliate TV stations (we called it a roadblock) in each of two selected isolated local markets—think Phoenix and Quad Cities, Iowa or Minneapolis and Charlotte. We would balance the market choices in demographics and brand development.

People would be called the next day to see if they were watching TV at the time the commercial ran, which was usually early fringe time, so time could be purchased as a local spot and not be in network time. If respondents were confirmed as watching, they were asked if they remembered any commercials. That response was what we called "unaided recall."

They were then asked if they recalled a commercial for a specific product. That was "aided recall" or "prompted recall." If they answered "yes," they were asked for specifics about the commercial—their fragmentary descriptions of what they recalled were recorded as "verbatims."

The bad news—all three of the JOP test commercial options, including Cosby, had average to below average DAR scores versus our norms.

Less than 20 percent of people who had been in the audience and had seen one of the commercials, even remembered it the next day. The Cosby option scored marginally better than the other two but not significantly. There were category and brand norms from previous DAR testing, and the test commercials did not score significantly different from the norms.

Just as these results came in, I was transferred to be the new account executive on JOP, now about a year and a half after the brand's television advertising had been suspended. We were faced with a decision on what to do.

The creative group was directed by Howard Rieger with Curvin O'Reilly as supervisor. The Cosby campaign was Curvin's brainchild, and he championed it. I had worked with Howard before as well as some of the teams that worked with him. I would often lobby to get teams I worked well with assigned to what I was working on. As a quite junior executive, I didn't have much leverage, but I tried to exercise what leverage I had. When you have folks you work well with, you want to work with them again. This was important in a company of more than 2,000 people, with a hundred or more creative teams. I hadn't worked with Curvin before, but this time, I was lucky to get other folks I already knew.

The Cosby commercials were very simple. They featured Bill Cosby sitting with a bunch of little kids about six years old on a simple set: a school classroom or a playroom. The kids and Cosby all have a bowl of JOP. Cosby tells a story to the kids about loving JOP and afterward they all happily eat their pudding.

Other GF brands had used celebrity spokespeople—some worked, and some did not. Either way, they were an expensive option due to the cost of the celebrity. The Cosby sets were simple and inexpensive. Curvin did a great job of writing copy that sounded like it came spontaneously out of Cosby's mouth. Cosby did a great job delivering the lines.

Despite the low DAR scores, our client agreed to put the Cosby commercial on air as a fill in, because the brand had not been on air for so long. Further, Cosby had some slightly richer recall verbatims, and there was the sunk cost of having paid him for the test commercials.

At the same time, we agreed with the client that the agency had to continue developing a replacement campaign that might test with better than just average DAR scores. We thought Cosby was strictly a stop-gap solution to keep JOP in the public awareness.

One of my next tasks was to finalize our contract with Bill Cosby through his agent, Norm Brokaw. We wanted easy options to get out of the contract in case we came up with an idea that tested better.

Cosby's contract provided him with a $100,000 per year fee with 10 percent increases in subsequent years. Not enormous or the highest celebrity endorsement fees, but significant in 1974 dollars. It would be worth about $500,000 in today's dollars. It was a lot for a small brand to bet on a spokesperson with no endorsement track record.

Cosby was a ground-breaking entertainer in terms of his color. If he had been a white entertainer, it is quite likely he would have made more; but that is just my guess. At the time, the actor playing Mr. Whipple for P&G was rumored to be making $300,000 per year to squeeze the Charmin toilet paper, but he had a few years of demonstrated success behind his campaign.

For our fee, we got a limited number of shooting days per year with Cosby. This meant that commercial productions had to be well planned so multiple commercials could be shot in a day, rather than a more normal one per day. When your celebrity is available, it is golden time, costly and not replaceable.

The fee was guaranteed against union double scale. Each time a network commercial runs, a payment would be accounted for at double the union scale rate for the airing. The union rates were calculated on geographic coverage, national, or spot (individual markets).

Each year, if the normal union talent payments at double scale exceeded $100,000, Cosby would get additional payments in the amount of that excess (I am giving you some of the details to show that talent contracts are not simple agreements, but can get quite complicated). Getting to that excess payment condition seemed like a long shot to us and was easy to include. With JOP's very low media budget, we thought it would never happen. During negotiation, you often grudgingly concede something that you think has little value, but that the other party thinks is very worthwhile.

We had dessert category exclusivity, meaning Cosby could not work with any other dessert; we did not have complete commercial exclusivity, that would have cost a lot more to offset any opportunity he would have lost. Like all contracts with known celebrities, there was a "moral turpitude" clause—in case of any scandal, the contract could be voided. This was a stock clause and had nothing to do with our ability to see more than 30 years into the future and anticipate Cosby's legal problems. Moral turpitude allowed for dissolution of the contract if either party did anything to embarrass the other.

For lack of better alternatives, we put the Cosby advertising on the air; but we had little confidence it was going to do anything for the brand.

We set about working on developing new advertising campaigns to test, to replace our temporary Cosby solution. I still have some of the key frames from this exercise in my files. Trying to increase sales of JOP was still a long-term problem that no one seemed to be able to solve. Pushing sales to retailers by shelf loading through promotions was one way, but we needed consumers to buy it off the-shelf as well.

Every two months, we would get AC Nielsen reports showing sales in grocery stores all around the country based on a predictive sample. About this time, something weird started to happen to JOP. Sales started going up, and not just a little, by as much as 25 percent in some markets.

In retrospect, we should have suspected that it was the advertising, but other brands with larger budgets had tried celebrity spokespeople, and some had been costly mistakes that brought weak results. All the team of professional marketers and advertising people believed, based on our pretesting, that the new JOP advertising was nothing special, a short-term solution, and it still needed to be replaced. It just did not seem to be such a big advertising idea.

The first time this sales bump showed up, the JOP product manager and his team hypothesized that it might just be a random blip, maybe statistical errors or some kind of sample correction from Nielsen since it hadn't happened before. An anomaly.

Similar growth in the next report caused us to think that it might have been due to a promotion program offering bonus cases to retailers. A promotion had been offered to load stores with inventory hoping to push product out. Or maybe one of our test market products (we had two going on for two packaging-based line extensions) was doing well enough to have increased sales. Could be...

But then it happened again. Sales were increasing on a brand where sales did not dramatically increase. Based on the brand's long-term sales history, even with a positive trend, it might have taken five years to increase as much as it had in the previous few months.

As the advertising advocate on the marketing team, I naturally claimed that it was the advertising—despite the poor pretest results. At first, my claim was considered to be just in the agency's self interest (it was). Nevertheless, we concluded that we should explore consumer responses to the commercials through some Focus Groups.

Group sessions were developed and scheduled for Atlanta. I recall it was Atlanta because I got lost among all the Peachtree Streets, Peachtree Avenues, Peachtree Drives, and so on, in my first trip to the city. Correctly executed, Focus Groups operate by keeping the participants blind to the research's goal to get more honest responses. Discussion started broadly: "Do you all prepare meals for your family"—slowly discussion narrowed in on our real subject—"so... do you prepare desserts as well?" This slow focusing in keeps participants from saying what they think we want to hear, as we close in on the subject as naturally as possible.

The term "Focus Group" has been misused recently. A session should start wide and allow the discussion to naturally narrow in, or focus, on the reason for the research. If respondents are aware of the reason for the study, they will say what they think we want to hear. We want reality not platitudes.

Off we went for a Focus Group in Atlanta to a facility on Peachtree something—are all the streets in Atlanta named Peachtree?

At the research facility, the JOP product management team and I stayed behind a one-way mirror in a darkened room. We were invisible observers of the sessions. In those days, the participants were totally unaware that the mirrors were one-way glass. Our proof that they were unaware was when one heavy-set woman in a polyester pant suit came in, checked herself very closely in the one-way mirror inches from our noses. Not an alluring close-up.

These Atlanta respondents were women who prepared meals for their families. Most were middle to lower middle class. Some worked out of the home, most not. All were preselected because they were JOP users; however, pudding would have been only one on a long list of products they were asked about when being recruited, leaving them unaware of what the session was about. We watched in our dark room behind our one-way mirror—ready to take notes on what they said.

Slowly the discussion wound its way to pudding. About halfway through the session, our moderator told the women that she was going to show a TV commercial. This was early on in videotape technology and required a video cassette machine that was not something they were familiar with.

Lights went out and the Cosby commercial was played on what today we would think of as a tiny TV screen. Lights came back on. The moderator asked if anyone had any questions. There was no response, but eventually one of the oversized ladies in polyester raised her hand and timidly asked "Can we see it again?"

Our moderator was not ready for this. She was expecting to start a discussion about the commercial. After some humming and hawing, the lights went down again. The commercial played again. This time, there were audible giggles in the room followed by another request to see it again. And then again. The commercial was played over and over and over, ignoring our allotted time schedule.

After about a half a dozen times, the moderator forced discussion. All the women in the room enthusiastically commented about how much fun the commercial was to watch, pointing out certain enjoyable details, the kids' eager consumption, their sideways looks for approval from Cosby, and the kids' reactions to Cosby, his expressions, his voices. The moms loved it.

In the darkened room behind the one-way mirror, our collective lights went on. People loved the commercials. Not liked. *Loved.*

You can't get that information from a one time, DAR test, which only asks the fast brain for some facts and how provocative it was.

We quickly concluded that the commercials were the reason for the sudden JOP sales spurt. It was our eureka moment, even though it came six months after deciding to put the commercials on the air as a temporary measure.

We immediately set to work on developing our next pool of three commercials featuring Bill Cosby. The expensive development of backup campaigns was put on hold at the agency. Soon after, the JOP advertising media spending budget was doubled.

Our occasional strokes of advertising genius often get muddled in the process they must go through to get approved. In this case, we bumbled into brilliance—despite the process.

This great creative idea boosted sales for more than 20 years, yet we, the experts at GF and Y&R, many with illustrious careers judging creative, assessing research, never saw it coming. None saw the full power of this simple idea.

Another lesson learned is that there are people behind all the decisions that get made. Those people have feelings and agendas that can change the outcomes. They also carry the preconceived notions about things such as how a brand responds to advertising.

How these ideas are viewed depends on the social context they are presented in. If our original client had not disliked the "too New York" Sheldon commercial so much, JOP might never have had a 20-year advertising run with Cosby.

A celebrity who is relevant to the product, whether the relevance is real or implied from the reasons for their celebrity, is more persuasive than one who is not relevant.

What made Cosby credible in delivering the JOP message was his relationship with kids. He became the spokesman for the kids telling moms that kids loved pudding.

His relevance came from his Fat Albert TV show, his personal "childlike" style of presenting, and the comedy routines where he empathized and told stories about his childhood. Based on these, people understood him to be a person who had a close relationship with kids and could talk to them effectively. Years later, he even hosted the "Kids Say the Darndest Things" TV show.

As for Cosby, the JOP campaign opened doors for him. He soon became a Coca Cola spokesman. This prompted me to call and try to convince his management that they should be cautious not to dilute his equity by doing too many commercials. Then he became the spokesman for IBM. It was a breakthrough for him and for people of color.

Today, many years have passed and Cosby has been disgraced. JOP is no longer a significant packaged good that can be found in everyone's household (we had about 85 percent plus household penetration at the time), having been supplanted by many more convenient products with the same sensory delivery that align better with busier working households.

Appreciation for this story of the power of the Cosby Jell-O advertising campaign will likely diminish as well. Sic transit gloria. Social context counts.

The story of this highly successful creative solution and the rigors it went through are not atypical. Doubt is easier to come by than belief in a solution. We don't always recognize an effective solution when we see it, even after the fact.

What made this campaign successful were several factors, some on purpose, some by luck.

First, it followed the strategy. It was the same strategy the previous campaigns had followed. Second, despite the recall test failure with the fast brain, only about 20 percent remembered it the next day; it was lucky to have been put on the air by the circumstance it was in.

Third, the campaign had credibility because Cosby was seen as an expert spokesperson for children based on his style and stories. The warmth and humor and familiarity with Cosby relaxed the fast brain. This friendly approach let the brand enter into the range of menu options for the consumers without too much resistance.

Jell-O became more salient and acceptable as a dessert option. Sales resulted.

The final factor in the campaign's success was that due to lack of alternatives, the advertiser had to be patient with the campaign. The campaign had all the strategic elements for success. The campaign was given a chance to establish itself as a warm and friendly brand message. You have to be good; you have to be lucky to get an opportunity; you have to make good on that opportunity. A great life lesson.

And we never saw it coming.

Stick to the fundamentals to succeed in the long run.

APPENDIX

Five Easy Pieces for Retailers

PART I: Running Redundant Advertising, Redundant Advertising

Our agency created advertising for retailers for years. But, we have always wondered why so many other retailers insist on repeating someone else's job.

Imagine—people who are notoriously careful with their funds—car dealers who haggle with their manufacturers in a tooth-and-nail duel, then turn around and do the same with customers. Then, they think the only thing they have to say about *their* dealership in *their* advertising is information about that same manufacturer's vehicles.

We have seen car dealers insist time after time: "Let's tell everyone about the new adjustable 'frammis pupjack 4.0' on the brand new 2024 model."

We say—NO! That is redundant! If you run redundant advertising, your dealership may become redundant. The manufacturer is already hyping the new "frammis pupjack 4.0"—why does the dealer have to do it too?

It is easy for retailers to make this mistake; it is top of mind because the manufacturer used it to tell them that sales will go up based on the incredible desirability of the new "frammis pupjack 4.0"—as proven in research.

Remember the discussion about primary and secondary demands. Primary demand is what brings people to the category; secondary demand brings them to your product. Since all dealers of a particular manufacturer will offer the same product, it is like a category benefit. Dealers need to stimulate secondary demand: preference for their dealership.

Like many industries, car advertising is neatly structured. The manufacturer spends their time speaking about the product. The food service industry is the same. The franchisor tells everyone about the product and service.

Let the national advertising provided by the manufacturer sing the praises of the products. That is their job. Let them promote the brand and all it stands for. After all, they own the brand; the franchisee retailer does not. If you are Conway Chevrolet, you own the Conway brand, not Chevrolet. Focus your messages in building the Conway brand.

Then let the dealer associations or franchisee co-ops talk about the shorter term group promotions: The BOGOs (Buy One Get One). The 0 percent interest financing. The employee pricing. These things benefit an entire group of retailers. No need for individual retailers to repeat these things since they all have the same offer. Reassure, yes. But feature, no. Even if your advertising is getting funds from the manufacturer to support the deal, lead with your brand.

Retailers should be advertising what makes their specific operation superb. Why service and deals at their dealership are the best. What their specific location can do for their customers. Focus advertising on special exclusive add-ons that only their store has. If there is no special added deal, there are other ways to stand out in a crowded field.

For car dealers, we recommend creating a personality for their dealership. This is no easy proposition. They need the kind of personality that appeals to their potential customers and is believable for that dealership. A personality lets customers feel they know that dealership and what that it stands for. Sometimes it is the dealer principal. But that is not the only choice.

This should be the emphasis, even when spending manufacturer advertising coop funds. Find a way to get your brand-selling idea into the message.

Even though they are franchises, car dealerships are big businesses and can afford to have their own business personality under their manufacturer signs. Not necessarily so for other types of franchisees.

Retailers should locally brand their store or dealership with store-specific ads that talk about their specific store. Many franchisors provide ads, and they help build the franchised brands collectively. But those do not do much for the local store; they do not separate a single store from the herd. A retailer using only franchisor-developed ads is penny wise and pound foolish.

Dealers and other retailers are not getting the most from their money unless they have something that adds uniqueness about their location—and we are not talking about just their address. Location equals convenience in our previous discussions.

Uniqueness could come from a special offer, promotion, event, or limited-edition model. Perhaps the company ad they get for free can be adapted to make it the location's own. Why would you run someone else's ad for your business?

For food service, we recommend that franchisees invest their own money in local store marketing. Each retailer needs traffic specifically at their location, so each needs to look for ways to build that traffic and extend their trading area. We wrote a book about it for franchisees we worked with, and it helped them when they took initiative. We recommended reaching out to groups that got together for meetings to create catering opportunities at schools, churches, offices, and community associations.

It can be as simple as reaching out to community associations and offering them a special deal for their members. It can be as simple as doing a speaking engagement to spread your name and location information.

There is so much that retailers can do to drive their own sales by connecting to and becoming involved in their communities. And it pays off.

For all retailers, presenting a personality and connecting to their community can be more effective than repeating whatever the national brand has to say.

Let the national brands do their job. Retailers, do yours—and build on the national advertising program as a base for your efforts.

PART II: What's More Important: Your Ego or Your Business?

Recently, I had a meeting with an accountant who does corporate turn-arounds. He attempts to save companies that are teetering on the brink of bankruptcy by nursing them back to health by using sound business practices.

I asked him whether some company owners put their ego ahead of the survival of their company. He said that was usually the biggest problem he faces in small-to-midsized businesses. Separating the ego from the business. Funny, I said, that is also a huge problem we encounter when we are doing advertising for retailers. And retailers are not alone.

The goal of operating a business is to make a profit. Without the profit, you cannot stay in business very long. Without retaining some earnings, you cannot weather a storm that will come, when there are setbacks. And there are bumps in the road for almost every company.

Even though some business owners can barely speak clearly, they take to the airwaves to hock their wares. Do they do it because they think they can deliver the message better than anyone else? More sincerely? More credibly?

We have a saying in advertising: If you haven't got anything to say, sing it. If you cannot sing it, get the client to say it themselves.

We do this to cater, maybe even pander, to the client's ego, because sometimes the client's ego is more important to them than business results. Besides, how can the client say "Fire the announcer" if it is them. They are invested in the advertising; they are pigs, not chickens.

By that I mean that when you have bacon and eggs for breakfast, the chicken is involved but the pig is committed. The chicken can walk away afterward. The pig cannot.

Of course, there are exceptions to this where the business operator can deliver a strong message. The Wendy's advertising problem mentioned earlier, led their founder to deliver a no-nonsense well-crafted message. It was supposed to be a short-term fall back; 20 years later, Dave Thomas was still doing them.

How was he successful? He happened to have the right personality, good copywriters to help, and the advertising persevered with him. He reminded everyone of a favorite, self-effacing uncle, not someone hawking his own wares. He was committed in a nonauthoritative way. His credibility came from his commitment and ownership, which overwhelmed the self-serving motivation. As time went on, we learned more about him and got to like him as his public personality was developed. He trusted his agency with the copy they wrote for him.

That is a far cry from retailers screaming out about some deal that they are offering. Dave was soft spoken and genuine. He seemed trustworthy and as the creator of the brand, he had expertise.

The best way to build a retail business is to understand your competitive set; understand your business advantage and develop intrusive, provocative, and clear advertising that communicates that strategy. What agency is going to tell the business owner, their client, to get off the air? That is the hard part for an agency. But it takes a smart client to trust in the copy the agency has written for them.

Retailers are not alone. We also see commercials that are all about the advertiser with little recognition for the customer. Who cares about an advertiser winning awards unless the awards are paid off in benefits for their customers. "We won this award five years running!!"—nice for you, now what's in it for me. Where's my WIIFM?

Retailers may know too much about their businesses to understand what is really compelling to their customers. Glimpses can be deceiving. We like to listen deeply to customers for a fairer assessment of a business's strengths and weaknesses. That takes some work and humility.

We spoke with a small QSR chain (that remains nameless) about their advertising. When we asked about customers, the owner told us her customers were fanatically loyal, which they seemed to be. Then we asked why she issued so many coupons. "We have to… to keep their business," she exclaimed. She did not see the disconnect—if the customers were loyal, they should not need to be bribed to keep coming back. Coupons provide an incentive for nonusers to try the product, or lapsed users to return. Rewarding people who would already come in is not a good use of your marketing funds. It can become a way of lowering your everyday price. She did not really know her customers, but bought into the sycophantic feedback she was getting.

Coupons can be addictive, as well. If you are rolling coupons out every month, be prepared for the sales drop when you stop. Coupons are like drugs and are hard to kick cold turkey.

When it comes to credibility, we believe that a customer saying how great a retailer is can provide a much stronger message than the retailer saying it themselves. We have discussed this before in the chapter about credibility. Think of it. If I tell you how great I am, you may be skeptical (although I have no idea why). Whereas if a disinterested third party says I am great, maybe even my wife will believe it. (OK, OK, there are limits to any theory.)

For most retailers, telling the prospects how great your company is yourself is not only the lazy, cheap way to do it but also one of the weakest. The retailer should ask themselves—which is more important, being recognized on the street or having your sales and revenue going up?

If they are their own spokesman, the retailer will get positive instore feedback that can be gratifying to their ego. It can make customers feel like they know you when they come in. The more important question is will it drive traffic into the store and make sales? Will the positive feedback, when people see you, distort your ability to see what makes your business tick.

The objective of advertising for your business is not to make you feel better, but to generate sales. Sales should generate the bottom-line profits that really make you feel better.

Don't use your advertising budget to make yourself more recognizable at cocktail parties, or have people stop you in the supermarket for an autograph. These don't deliver sales unless the story you have been telling brings people real benefits, they feel they are connected, and they can trust what you are saying. It should be like winning awards for advertising agencies, nice but unintended. A map can bring in more customers than an owner's sparkling teeth.

We have worked with a lot of owners; they are successful people with a lot of confidence. They have needed it to get where they are. It is hard for them to take a back seat on anything.

Unless the retailer has a particular talent or uniqueness, stay away from this type of advertising! This technique can only lead to problems. And it is the second common mistake that retailers make.

PART III: Ads Filled With Information but No Persuasive Message

Some ads from retailers, especially newspaper ads, make understanding the DaVinci code or the plot in an Avenger movie a simple thing. The ads are complicated, incomplete… leaving potential customers puzzled.

These ads assume that if you throw an entire vegetable garden at the wall, it will somehow magically become an excellent marinara sauce. We looked at one for a prominent auto dealer recently and stopped counting type fonts and claims when we ran out of fingers and toes. There was everything from how many languages the staff spoke, to illegible descriptions about all kinds of cars, to loan conditions with the attendant legal caveats in tiny text, and so on.

Having that many claims indicates that no one could decide which one would really work; there was no copy strategy. It screams out "We specialize in everything!"— which means you specialize in nothing. We devoted an entire chapter to honing a copy strategy to single-mindedness.

We sympathize with the poor customer who tries to figure out what these bingo cards for an ad are supposed to communicate. Think of a dictionary—it has all the words, but no plot. That is exactly how some ads are. They have lost the plot.

We assume that the normal customer has a small little memory space in their brain to connect an advertiser with what they stand for. The customer can connect one or two and maybe three ideas to that advertiser, not much more. What are those one, two, or three words that are associated with your retail store?

Consider how effective arguments are made. Once you get past one or two good reasons for your point, your argument gets weaker. There is no bell (see the Nobel Prize story further on in the Appendix). That is enough.

When a consumer is given 20 or more sales points, they can not only refute many of them but also disbelieve many of them. The additional points do not add value to the persuasiveness of the ad, they undermine it. We have already discussed many examples of this.

What is more effective and memorable? A single strong claim with believable, tangible support or a rambling list of questionable assertions?

When you only have a few seconds to make your impression, you better be clear and make your point compelling.

Shooting elephants with shotguns makes the elephants mad and confused, but it will hardly be a successful hunt.

As Michelangelo said, "Every block of stone has a statue inside it, and it is the task of the sculptor to discover it." The same is true for finding the right advertising message.

Retailers tend to deliver the block of stone and expect the customer to do the sculpting. It is a risky and inefficient way to advertise.

If they are afraid to leave something out, they are not alone. Many advertisers try to cram every possible positive point about their products into their advertising.

I experienced this with the fax machines that we advertised years ago. There were so many features to feature that we could not keep straight how these features all worked. If they were that obscure to us who were deeply focused on the product, they could not really be meaningful to prospective buyers—except for a very select few. I never did figure out what "polling" was on these fax machines.

Retailers who identify their key message and stick to it have the best opportunity to stand apart from their competitors and build a reputation for themselves. Reputations that are consistent build relationships, familiarity, and credibility.

That message should focus on one defining difference from their competitors. The message should motivate their customers with a clear benefit to those customers. The retailer should also make sure that they can deliver the benefit. If you say your food is "Hot and Fresh," you better deliver on that promise.

Sounds easy. So does Michelangelo's task—"You just chip away the stone that does not look like David." We know the hardest thing about a creative strategy for the advertiser is what you leave out. Too much information usually means no clear compelling message at all.

PART IV: What the Media Is Selling— What You Are Buying

We will avoid textbook definitions of GRPs, reach and frequency, impressions, CPP and CPM; let's get to the point. There is a difference between what media people sell and what advertising people want to buy.

A car dealer is selling metal, plastic, rubber, leather, and electronics; their customer is buying transportation, comfort, and perhaps some status. A restaurant is selling vegetables, meats, grains, and service; their customer is buying a meal. A clothing retailer is selling fabric, design, and assembled clothes; their customer is buying good looks, confidence, and a comfortable fit.

The same is true of media. The media is selling announcements, copies of publications, placement of ads, and programing. What the retailer should be buying are impressions, eyeballs, and audience. Who cares about the paper or the broadcast signal?

Retailers often erroneously assume that their media preferences are the same as their customers' preferences. If they listen to a particular radio station or watch a television station or show, that means everyone else does. In a subtle way, this is also putting their ego ahead of their business.

In larger metro areas, the media choices are extensive. The retailer who makes self-oriented kinds of media choices for their advertising should be prepared when results are poor. Their friends may all see it, but the potential customers are the more important ones. The retailers' customers are not like them; the customers don't own retail outlets, for one.

From car dealers to fast food operators, clothing stores to services, almost every retailer we have ever dealt with (literally hundreds) thinks media buying is about how many spots or insertions you can get for a given price.

That brings us to the whole point about media. Buying media is about buying what we mentioned: impressions, eyeballs, and audience. It is not about seeing how many spots you can get. You buy eyes and ears to get to the audience's fast brains.

The reason some print vehicles or radio or TV stations cost much more to advertise in than others is because of their audiences—much,

much more audience. It is the same reason you pay much more rent for a store on Main Street than Mud Street.

When you think about retail traffic, think about audiences. Also consider the quality of the media to make sure your message is associated with the correct environment. Like getting the right location for a retail store, buying media is about audience, audience, audience.

Evaluate how much audience there is, not how many times your ad will be printed or aired. Printing a million copies that don't get distributed or read does the advertiser no good. Airing 10 commercials in the overnight usually isn't worth one in prime time. You want audience. Don't confuse process with results; it is easy to be distracted by action, whether it helps or not.

Retailers also love perks. Media salespeople know this very well. Media packages for retailers are often packaged up with personal perks for the retailer: tickets, trips, and other entertainment. The costs for these are embedded in the advertising package, so these funds are siphoned off from the ad budget and are not creating sales impact, except for the media.

Retailers—ask yourself whether your personal enjoyment is worth the trade-off from your business. Then reread the previous section about whether your ego is more important than your business. When you compromise, understand that you have diverted your benefits. Do not expect a win–win.

PART V: Seek Professional Help for Advertising

Ever go into a car dealership and ask the sales guy to tune your engine? You don't really think that they would know how to do it, do you? They know their limitations.

Salespeople sell cars; they do not provide highly technical engine adjustments. The dealership has trained mechanics for that. And the mechanics don't try to sell cars.

Everyone develops a skill set and has certain talents. We call on experts, or those more expert than we are, to complete tasks we are less proficient at. Except for the Duanes of the world who can take out their own appendices.

We do not do our own open-heart surgery, our own dentistry, or usually our own taxes. Maybe Duane does.

Why do smaller businesses think that they are experts at creating advertising campaigns? Is it because they think they can speak English, so they believe they can write copy? Does watching TV make you an expert in media buying? Just because something looks like an ad, does not make it real advertising.

Once I cold-called a prospect who had ineffective advertising I had heard. I asked him who wrote his advertising copy. He said he was very happy having his secretary do it (back in the day when people had secretaries). To which I replied that secretary was underutilized. "Has your secretary thought about writing screenplays, there is more money in that." I am an inveterate smartass. Anyone who was proud of bad advertising is unlikely to ask for help.

Maybe someone in-house is a great copywriter, undiscovered and instinctive. It could happen. Also, people could understand my sarcasm. Neither is likely.

The power of having the right advertising campaign is not something left to amateurs. In *Outliers* by Malcolm Gladwell, he endorses the idea that someone needs to have 10,000 hours of purposeful practiced learning doing something before they become expert at it. Once an expert, you can get the benefit of that expertise in a blink! If you have read this far, you should have a good idea of the framework necessary to do this, even if you don't have the writing skills of that prospect's secretary. That framework allows you to judge the work, but not necessarily create it.

Advertising agencies have well-developed and disciplined processes for the development of creative ads. Hopefully, we have covered most of them here. We define a strategy beforehand to make sure we are putting forward the right message to the right target. It takes years of training to get this right. The power of having the right message in the right place can increase the impact of the media investment in many multiples.

What does it take for a retailer to gain this benefit? The courage to ask for professional help.

Some retailers are afraid of the cost. Really? Any professional service should pay for itself.

They should ask: "How much money are we wasting by not having a powerful message?" "Are we confusing action with progress?"

Retailers are usually great at operations, making sure their stores operate consistently and efficiently. They focus on themselves in doing this.

Advertising people are trained to think differently. They think starting from the customers' point of view. This means that when a retailer hires an advertising professional, the advice they get is a feedback loop, a translation of what the retailer is doing into customer talk.

The retailer should ask the question, "Does this achieve what I am trying to do?" instead of the more typical question, "Is that how I would do it myself?"—Of course, it is *not* how you would do it! That is why you hired an expert with a different perspective.

It is the wise person who knows what they can and cannot do. Professional advertising advice can pay for itself and then some.

I have my own appendectomy to do. Now, where did I put my chainsaw?

One More Tip for the Road

So many retailers voice their own commercials that these commercials are ubiquitous. They are also generally not very good.

Our cynical view of their body of work, led us to these top 10 reasons why retailers voice their own commercials:

1. They are "owners" and have big egos already.
2. They work cheap.
3. The client (themselves) loves the talent selection (themselves).
4. The retailers are intrinsically identified with their business or dealership (often their name is already on the sign).
5. It is easy to get approval for the production.
6. Their competitors all do it, so they think it is normal.
7. Otherwise, they do not have anything relevant to say about their dealership.
8. The copywriting may be bad, but it is cheap, and the talent is allowed to go off script.
9. It gets them on TV for added PR value. When the station has an industry-related question, as an advertiser, they may be called and that creates more awareness.
10. Their relatives and friends compliment them at parties and dinners.

Notice how few, if any, of these have anything to do with communicating a message that can help to build their business.

Retailers are naturally impatient with any advertising message. Time is perishable; a sale lost yesterday cannot be regained.

When retailers, themselves, are the talent, it can be burdensome to make frequent commercial changes unless they are willing to go into a studio regularly. We have seen some situations where the staff are happy to get the business's principal distracted or out of the place of business for any reason, and recording commercials is as good an excuse as any.

For radio, many retailers just phone in their performance—literally. They phone the radio studio or station and have their voice recorded off the phone. And creatively, of course, this approach is also just "phoning in" the creative without being fully prepared. It often ends with a babbling commercial rather than hitting the sales points needed.

There is a weakness to the marketing strategy that says: "I am the business." When the time comes to sell the business, their media personalities are part of the equity.

We worked with one dealer who understood that we wrote better copy and often commented, "Where do you get this stuff from?" We gave him a "Greatest Hits" CD with his face on the cover after we had done more than 100 commercials with him.

Occasionally, we would include commercials for him that did not sell a particular offer but gave some positive insight into his persona, like why he wore his college tie and so forth. We were building his integrity in the process. The more people think they know and are familiar with you, the more credibility you have, the more they trust you.

When he sold the dealership, he had to provide continuity based on his name and radio persona.

Sometimes voicing your own commercials works fine. The hard part is listening to people who know objectively to make sure your message is right. Then taking the time to make sure your script has the content and charm to make it effective.

Fast Brain Fallacy: How Many Countries in Africa?

A couple of years ago, I gave an in-class presentation to a group of mature students about the psychology used in advertising that leads people to deceive themselves.

At the end of the class, a few, okay a majority of students, said that they did not believe me. These mature students said they could never be fooled by these techniques… and besides, they were not influenced by advertising at all. They always made rational decisions.

Before their next class a week later, I contacted the teacher and asked him to put a large number 19 on the blackboard before anyone got there and not to mention anything about it. I just chose a random, prime number that was low enough to make my point.

The teacher did as he had been asked and the 19 sat there amidst the clutter of notes at the far end of the blackboard when students arrived for class. No one mentioned it.

I attended as a follow-up.

About half an hour into the class, I asked if I could address some of the doubts that had arisen from my presentation at the previous class; how people felt that they were smart enough never to be fooled by psychological techniques.

I spoke for a few moments to rebut some of the issues that had been brought up in my presentation the previous week. This was to distract and relax them, get them off their guard. Then, I announced I would do a demonstration. I asked everyone, including the teacher, to take out a pen and a small piece of paper.

I said I had a quick question; there were no marks involved. I just wanted each of them to give me their best guess and write it immediately on the little scrap of paper. The question was "How many countries are there in Africa?"

I had picked a subject that had a specific quantitative answer, but was obscure enough I thought no one would know the answer.

I immediately started to collect their answers giving them no time to think, so they had to rely only on their fast brain. There were groans and protests. They had no time to even count on their fingers, just write a number on a slip of paper. The first number that came to mind.

I collected the 20 or so slips of paper and asked the teacher to help do a distribution of the answers right then on the blackboard in front of everyone. The distribution showed answers tightly clustered from 18 to 21 with one outlier answer in the 30s.

I asked the class if they believed in the wisdom of crowds. That is, if no one person knows an answer, if you ask a group, are they likely, as a group, to estimate correctly? Many thought this suggestion made a lot of sense. It is, after all, the basis of our democratic election systems. It is, perhaps, a demonstration of regression to the mean.

Then, I asked why they thought their answers clustered around 19 or 20?

They agreed that it must be because it was the correct answer, more or less. This was me exploiting an overt suggestion I had just made about the wisdom of crowds. I had given them a reason to believe that as a group they were better at estimating than any one of them. It is also an example of confirmation bias—they had all (except one) just given answers in that range. Now they had some rationale to believe in the correctness of their behavior.

If you direct people's thinking, they will follow along without engaging their slow brain. In psychological experiments and in surveys, this directing is called creating expectancy. People are willing to give you what they think you want if it does not cost them anything and reduces their dissonance or anxiety. Unfortunately, it can distort experimental or survey results and make them useless.

Then, I pointed to the number 19 over on a corner of the blackboard near the window and asked if anyone noticed the number. Most claimed not to have noticed it.

I asked, "If no one noticed it, why did it so strongly influence the group's answers that all clustered around 19?" They suggested that one had nothing to do with the other.

I pointed out that in this case, there was an actual quantifiable number we could measure against. There are 54 countries in Africa. They were surprised; they started to think about it logically. They began counting countries on their fingers as their slow brain became engaged to confirm what I had said. Most of them quickly got past 19 countries and kept going.

The trick in creating this bias was to keep people using the fast part of their brain that keeps track of what is happening in the here and now. Not allowing them to use the slow part of the brain that stores accumulated learning. I had picked the question because the answer was not commonly known, thereby creating the need for a guess from the fast brain.

If you need a response quickly, the response will most likely be what you most recently saw or heard. It is called recency bias. That's why repetition helps solidify brand names for quick response at the shelf. If a brand is the last one a customer heard, they default to it.

The class might have denied that they had even seen the number 19, but the evidence was striking. It was the last number they saw before I asked the question, and I did not give them time to think through their response. It was amazing how strongly influential the unspoken suggestion was on them.

We are all influenced in ways we are not so consciously aware of. It isn't subliminal; it is because the fast brain is lazy.

The Nobel Prize Winning Creative Strategy

The bishop arrives by train one morning for his first visit to an old walled medieval town. The townspeople knew he was coming. He is greeted by the local priest and the town's mayor who express gratitude and honor for the visit.

The bishop is taken to the town square where all the townspeople have gathered. Speeches are made and the children put on an historical pageant. The bishop is then escorted to the town hall where there is a fine and ample lunch prepared by the people of the town.

Following the lunch, there is a full church service for the bishop where all the citizens show up dressed in their finest clothes. The service is followed that evening by a banquet and a concert with singers and dancers from the town.

As the local priest escorts the bishop back to the train for the bishop's return to his home, the priest asks the bishop how he enjoyed his day.

The bishop is effusive in his compliments for the food, service, pageantry… everything. "But" he says, "I have one question. Usually when I visit a town for the first time, they ring the bells in the church. Why did you not do so?"

"I knew you would ask that," said the local priest unfurling a long sheet of responses.

"I have here a list of 37 reasons why we did not." And with that he rapidly begins to rattle them off: "First, we have no bells. Second, we were unsure of the most appropriate melody. Third, we were…."

"Wait!" said the bishop, "What did you say the first reason was?"

"We… have no bells." stuttered the local priest.

"That's good enough." replied the bishop, "One good reason is worth more than the other 36."

When you are making an argument, the third or fourth reason why your premise is convincing is usually weaker with the potential to undermine your whole premise. The listener seizes on those weaker support points to argue back against them in their heads. The more reasons you give, the weaker your argument becomes.

One good reason can win the "No Bell" prize.

Notes

Chapter 1

1. Goldberg (2013).

Chapter 2

1. Zillmann, Katcher, and Milavsky (1972), pp. 247–259.
2. Kahneman (2011).

Chapter 3

1. McGuire and Papageorgis (1961), pp. 327–337.
2. Chabris and Simons (2010).

Chapter 4

1. Steinbeck (1958), pp. 110–114.

Chapter 6

1. Mischel (2014).

Chapter 10

1. Wolfe (2023).

References

Chabris, C. and D. Simons. 2010. *The Invisible Gorilla, How Our Intuitions Deceive Us.* Harmony.

Goldberg, F.S. 2013. *The Insanity of Advertising: Memoirs of a Mad Man.* Council Oak Books.

Kahneman, D. 2011. *Thinking, Fast and Slow.* Farrar, Straus and Giroux.

McGuire, W.J. and D. Papageorgis. 1961. "The Relative Efficacy of Various Types of Prior Belief-Defense in Producing Immunity Against Persuasion." *The Journal of Abnormal and Social Psychology* 62, no. 2, pp. 327–337.

Mischel, W. 2014. *The Marshmallow Test: Mastering Self-Control.* Little, Brown and Company.

Steinbeck, J. 1958. "How to Tell Good Guys From Bad Guys." In *Ideas in Context*, ed. J. Satin. Houghton Miflin, pp. 110–114.

Wolfe, M. September 22, 2023. *Measuring the Long-Term Effects of Advertising.* LinkedIn.

Zillmann, D., A.H. Katcher, and B. Milavsky. 1972. "Excitation Transfer From Physical Exercise to Subsequent Aggressive Behavior." *Journal of Experimental Social Psychology* 8, pp. 247–259.

About the Author

Launched into life in Vancouver, BC, Canada, he was given the brand name **Barry Milavsky**. He graduated from the University of British Columbia and then did graduate work at the University of Pennsylvania receiving an MA in Communications. As a student, he worked in the summers as a prospector in Alaska and northern British Columbia.

On graduation from Penn, he immediately began work at Young & Rubicam on Madison Avenue in New York. He also worked at Benton & Bowles, NY, before joining Grey Advertising in Caracas, Venezuela, and then Grey in Toronto. He joined Canadian agency Ronalds–Reynolds, was a board director, and helped the company rapidly grow with business gains until it was purchased by FCB-Publicis.

He then started his own agency that he branded Calexis. Calexis worked with clients in the United States, Canada, and Australia including Subway, Chubb Insurance, Molson, Sunoco, Parmalat, and many others in sports, events, retail, energy, and food service. Calexis was the first agency in Canada on the Internet in 1994.

He has authored many industry articles, lectured at several universities, and given keynote speeches. He has served on industry boards, committees, and panels.

Index

OTHER TITLES IN THE MARKETING COLLECTION

Naresh Malhotra, Georgia Tech, Editor

- *Proximity Marketing* by Rajagopal
- *Winning With Strategic Marketing* by David Altounian and Mike Cronin
- *Brand Positioning With Power* by Robert S. Gordon
- *Multicultural Marketing Is Your Story* by Eliane Karsaklian
- *Marketing of Consumer Financial Products* by Ritu Srivastava
- *The Big Miss* by Zhecho Dobrev
- *Digital Brand Romance* by Anna Harrison
- *Brand Vision* by James Everhart
- *Brand Naming* by Rob Meyerson
- *Fast Fulfillment* by Sanchoy Das
- *Multiply Your Business Value Through Brand & AI* by Rajan Narayan
- *Branding & AI* by Chahat Aggarwal
- *The Business Design Cube* by Rajagopal
- *Customer Relationship Management* by Michael Pearce
- *The Coming Age of Robots* by George Pettinico and George R. Milne
- *Market Entropy* by Rajagopal

Concise and Applied Business Books

The Collection listed above is one of 30 business subject collections that Business Expert Press has grown to make BEP a premiere publisher of print and digital books. Our concise and applied books are for...

- Professionals and Practitioners
- Faculty who adopt our books for courses
- Librarians who know that BEP's Digital Libraries are a unique way to offer students ebooks to download, not restricted with any digital rights management
- Executive Training Course Leaders
- Business Seminar Organizers

Business Expert Press books are for anyone who needs to dig deeper on business ideas, goals, and solutions to everyday problems. Whether one print book, one ebook, or buying a digital library of 110 ebooks, we remain the affordable and smart way to be business smart. For more information, please visit www.businessexpertpress.com, or contact sales@businessexpertpress.com.

9 781637 426104